ONE NATION UNDER GOD?

BIBLE PROPHECY—WHEN THE AMERICAN EXPERIMENT FAILS

CLIFFORD GOLDSTEIN

Pacific Press Publishing Association
Boise, Idaho
Oshawa, Ontario, Canada

Edited by B. Russell Holt
Designed by Tim Larson
Cover photo by Sinclair Studios©
Typeset in 11/13 Janson Text

Copyright © 1996 by
Pacific Press Publishing Association
Printed in the United States of America
All Rights Reserved

Accuracy of all quotations and references is the responsibility of the author.

Goldstein, Clifford.
    One nation under God? : Bible prophecy—when the American experiment fails / Clifford Goldstein.
        p.   cm.
    Includes bibliographical references.
    ISBN 0-8163-1308-3 (alk. paper)
    1. Freedom of religion—United States. 2. Bible—Prophecies—Freedom of religion—United States. 3. Persecution—United States. 4. United States—Religion—1960-   5. Seventh-day Adventists—Doctrines. I. Title.
BR516.G58 1996
323.44'2'0973—dc20   95-26114
                                                          CIP

96 97 98 99 00 • 5 4 3 2 1

CONTENTS

INTRODUCTION

"In the face of the anti-Christ," wrote German theologian Dietrich Bonhoeffer, "only one thing has force and permanence, and that is Christ Himself."

As Seventh-day Adventists, we stand in the face of the antichrist. Whether persecution comes in two months or two decades, it hardly matters. What matters is that antichrist—the beast that prowls across the pages of Scripture from Daniel to Revelation—moves toward its apocalyptic destiny. Thus, Adventists move toward theirs as well.

Being Adventists in the last days is, in a macabre sense, somewhat like a person about to commit suicide. She knows just how the final period that ends her story will come. Adventists, too, know how that last punctuation mark will fall; they just don't type it in themselves.

One Nation Under God? doesn't concentrate on that final punctuation mark, though; instead, it deals with the last few lines before it, particularly those concerning the lamblike beast of Revelation 13 and its role in the final crisis.

"One nation, and only one, meets the specification of this prophecy," Ellen White wrote in *The Great Controversy* more than a century ago. "It points unmistakably to the United States of America" (440).

The United States has, from the beginning, been a noble experiment. Unfortunately, according to the "sure work of prophecy" (2 Peter 1:19), the experiment fails, even miserably. This book looks at how easily that failure, in the light of our understanding of Revelation, could happen.

One Nation Under God?, like *The Day of the Dragon* a few years before it, affirms the three angels' scenario, particularly the part about America's apocalyptic denouement. In the few years since publication of *The Day of the Dragon*, so many things of apparent prophetic significance have transpired that another book is needed to bring us up to date. *One Nation Under God?* attempts to do just that.

Adventists could look at recent political religious events, both in the United States and abroad, and be forgiven for almost believing that world religious and political leaders have read *The Great Controversy* and are determined to follow its script. That's how close the scenario is being played out. All one has to do, for example, is scan the papal encyclical *Ut Unum Sint*—John Paul's gut-wrenching call for Christian unity, issued in the summer of 1995— to see what I'm talking about. Even more to the point, the document *Catholics and Evangelicals Together: The Christian Mission in the Third Millennium* is one of the most powerful affirmations of our prophetic scenario. This book looks at some of these events and shows why we, as Adventists, have more reasons than ever to trust in the truths with which we, ourselves, have been entrusted.

Yet, ironically enough, *One Nation Under God?* affirms our prophetic truths by destroying many of our political ones.

In the previous century, seeking to annihilate the basic values of Western civilization, Frederick Nietzsche wrote that "your thoughts are not your experiences; they are an echo and aftereffect of your experiences; as when your room trembles when a carriage goes past. I, however, am sitting in that carriage, and often I am the carriage itself."

This book attempts to be that carriage, shaking—even undermining—many of the beliefs about religious freedom, separation of church and state, and the U.S. Constitution that Adventists harbor.

Why? Because many of those beliefs are, quite simply, wrong.

Our freedoms, religious liberties, even separation of church and state, don't necessarily rest on the rock that many Adventists think they do. Instead, they sit on constantly shifting, shaking, and eroding sediment. Almost all our presuppositions about American rights, liberties, and constitutional protections are fraught with contradictions, inaccuracies, and fallacies that the enemies of freedom know about and exploit. *One Nation Under God?* exposes these problems so that the reader can see for herself just how fragile liberty really is, and, thus, how easily American could fulfill its prophetic role. Indeed, considering these inherent weaknesses, it must be only by the grace of God that the lamblike beast hasn't yet spoken like a dragon.

"Whatever the importance of our understanding religious liberty questions now," I write in the last chapter, "particularly in the realm of church-state separation, and however crucial for Adventists to stand behind their religious liberty leaders during this struggle—in the final crunch, we can't lean on James Madison, the Constitution, and American history to defend our positions because neither Madison, the Constitution, nor American history always do."

As a matter of fact, a lot of things don't—except one, and that is the Word of God. This, my latest book, attempts to affirm us in the Word, particularly the prophetic understanding that Seventh-day Adventists—under the guidance of the Spirit—have brought to it for more than 150 years.

Clifford Goldstein
Columbia, Maryland
1995

"When the leading churches of the United States, uniting upon
such points of doctrine as are held by them in common,
shall influence the state to enforce their decrees and to sustain
their institutions, then Protestant America will have formed
an image of the Roman hierarchy, and the infliction of civil
penalties upon dissenters will inevitably result"
(Ellen White, *The Great Controversy*, 445).

"And now I have told you before it come to pass, that,
when it is come to pass, ye might believe"
(Jesus Christ, John 14:29).

"Meet Ralph Reed, 33. His Christian Coalition is on a crusade
to take over U.S. politics—and it's working"
(Time, Cover, 15 March 1995).

CHAPTER
ONE

"The Pope is not and cannot be the head of the Christian church and cannot be God's or Christ's vicar. Instead he is the head of the accursed church of all the worst scoundrels on earth, a vicar of the devil, an enemy of God, an adversary of Christ, a destroyer of Christ's churches; an arch church-thief and church robber of the keys of all the good of both the church and the temporal lords; a murderer of kings and inciter of bloodshed; a brothel-keeper over all brothel-keepers and all vermin, even that which can't be named; an anti-Christ, a man of sin" (Martin Luther, *Against the Roman Papacy As an Institution of the Devil*).

"Evangelicals and Catholics are brothers and sisters in Christ" (*Evangelicals and Catholics Together: The Christian Mission in the Third Millennium*).

"The future of American politics lies in the growing strength of Evangelicals and their Roman Catholic allies. If these two core constituencies—evangelicals comprising the swing vote in the South, Catholics holding sway in the North—can cooperate on issues and support like-minded candidates, they can determine the outcome of almost any election in the nation. Nasty nativism and dark distrust about Popery and foreign influence have been swept into the ash heap of history. John F. Kennedy's election in 1960 buried the Catholic bogeyman forever. No longer burdened by the past, Roman Catholics, evangelicals, Greek Orthodox, and many religious conservatives from the mainline denominations are forging a new alliance that promises to be among the most powerful and important in the modern political era" (Ralph Reed, Christian Coalition director, *Politically Incorrect*, 16).

When Jesus prayed that His people would be "one" (John 17:21), He wanted this unity to be based on truth, not politics. Yet politics, not truth, was behind the document *Evangelicals and Catholics Together: The Christian Mission in the Third Millennium*, signed by forty prominent American Catholic and evangelical leaders at the Institute of Religion and Public Life in New York City in early 1994.[1] The result of dialogue between American Catholic and evangelical leaders, the document represents an unprecedented breakthrough in relations between two historical enemies. With signatories ranging from John Cardinal O'Connor to tongues-speaking Pat Robertson, the document is proof that the Adventist prophetic scenario is unfolding.

"If this controversial document is any indication," wrote evangelical scholar Alister E. McGrath in *Christianity Today*, "there is every reason to think that there is a lessening of suspicion on both sides of the evangelical-Catholic gulf and a growing awareness of the possibilities for working together, as well as the dangers of not doing so."[2] (Notice McGrath's use of the word *gulf*.)

Though the New Right normally promotes religion under the guise of politics, *Evangelicals and Catholics Together* promotes politics under the guise of religion. Despite denials that the document represents a "partisan"[3] political agenda, it is nothing but politics, now cloaked under such religious verbiage as "the Christian mission in world history faces a moment of daunting opportunity and responsibility"[4] or such as "our unity in the love of Christ will become ever more evident as a sign to the world of God's reconciling power" (ibid., 7, 8).

Forget the religion fluff. The bottom line is that conservative Catholics and Protestants, particularly evangelicals, have united in the past decade in the United States on issues such as abortion, education vouchers, pornography, family values, and other common civil and political goals. The document admits that abortion in particular is what has brought Catholics and conservative Protestants together. "The pattern of convergence and cooperation between Evangelicals and Catholics is, in large part, a result of common effort to protect human life, especially the lives of the most vulnerable among us" (ibid., 15).

One slight problem: for centuries these churches, at least institutionally, have hated each other with a venom surpassed only by their hatred of Jews. They have either burned each other at the stake, condemned each other to burn in hell, or both, for almost half a millennium. Now suddenly they find themselves, in America at least, united on a common political agenda, even though they have never worked out the vast theological differences between them.

Evangelicals and Catholics Together attempts to deal with this theological divide by not dealing with it at all; instead, the document simply admits that though Catholics and evangelicals have differences, they can still accept each other as Christians and unite politically.

"We do not presume to suggest that we can resolve the deep and long standing differences between Evangelicals and Catholics," the document says. "Indeed these differences may never be resolved short of the Kingdom Come. Nonetheless, we are not permitted simply to resign ourselves to differences that divide us from one another" (ibid., 9).

Evangelicals and Catholics Together then lists some of the theological differences "that are frequently thought to divide us." These include such "trivia" as the authority of Scripture or of "Scripture as authoritatively interpreted in the church"; sacraments as symbols of grace or as a "means of grace"; "the priesthood of all believers" or ministry ordered in apostolic succession; the Lord's Supper as a "memorial meal" or a eucharistic sacrifice; and the "devotion to Mary and the saints" (ibid., 9, 10).

These represent vast theological divides, not just semantic ambiguities that a little dialogue among back-slapping theologians sitting in a committee room can resolve. The question of final authority in biblical interpretation is of major consequence. Either Mary is a dead woman, or she is, as wrote Catholic theologian Edward Schillebeeckx, "the Mediatrix between Christ and us."[5] Whether salvation is through faith alone or with the sacraments as well cuts to the essence of Christianity. Whether or not Christians need an institutional church to mediate between them and God involves the most basic issues of salvation.

If these issues simply represent "legitimate diversity,"[6] why have Catholics and evangelicals murdered each other for centuries over them? Teachings such as the sacrifice of the Mass and the use of sacraments are either Christian or anti-Christian. "The Catholic Church," wrote Cardinal Manning, "is either the masterpiece of Satan or the kingdom of the Son of God."[7] Cardinal Newman wrote that "a sacerdotal order is historically the essence of the Church of Rome; if not divinely appointed, it is doctrinally the essence of antichrist."[8]

How, then, could conservative Protestants sign a statement claiming that "we reject any appearance of harmony that is purchased at the price of truth"?[9] Whose truth? The Catholic or evangelical version, each of which is radically opposed to the other in crucial areas of soteriology, ecclesiology, and eschatology? Said the document:

> Whatever may be the future form of the relationship between our communities, we can, we must, and we will begin now the work required to remedy what we know to be wrong in that relationship. Such work requires trust and understanding, and trust and understanding require an assiduous attention to truth.[10]

Nonsense. Both sides are putting aside any "assiduous attention to truth" in order to justify their political alliances. Do the Protestants who signed the document—Southern Baptists, such as Doctors Richard Land and Larry Lewis,[11] or conservatives, such as Chuck Colson and Pat Robertson—truly believe that they have "unity in Christ" with those who pray to Mary or who teach that the literal body and blood of Christ, His "real presence," appears in the sacrifice of the Mass? What self-respecting Protestant believes that "the Christian mission is one"[12] with those who think they need an earthly priest to intercede between them and God? Far from a quest for truth, the document evades it as much as possible.

The statement has one section titled "WE AFFIRM TOGETHER," which deals with the theological points that Catholics and evangelicals can "affirm together." Out of the twenty-five-page document, this section takes less than four pages (which shows how much Catholics and evangelicals can really "affirm together").

They affirm together that "Jesus Christ is Lord."[13] With all due respect, Satan believes that. So did David Koresh. As Jesus said, "Many will say unto me on that day, Lord, Lord, have we not prophesied in thy name? and in thy name have cast out devils? and in thy name done many wonderful works? And then I will profess unto them, I never knew you" (Matthew 7:22, 23). Thomas Torquemada, the Grand Inquisitor, believed that Jesus Christ is Lord, even as he stretched victims on the rack.

They affirm together that "we are justified by grace through faith because of Christ" (ibid.). About six lines are devoted to that topic (three of which are a Bible quote), but not one word explains what being "justified by grace" means. That is probably because it means radically different things to Catholics and Protestants, especially since Roman Catholics teach that a priest must mediate justification—a teaching repulsive to Protestantism.

"We affirm together that Christians are to teach and live in obedience to the divinely inspired Scriptures, which are the infallible Word of God" (ibid., 6). But how are Christians to live in obedience to the Bible when they are miles apart on what it means or on who has the final authority in interpreting it? Mormons and Jehovah's Witnesses say that they live in obedience to the Bible. So do members of Dallas's Cathedral of Hope, the world's largest gay church. The statement means nothing.

"We further affirm together that Christ has promised to his church the gift of the Holy Spirit who will lead us into all truth in discerning and declaring the teaching of Scripture" (ibid.). But how could the Holy Spirit have been leading both communions into "all truth" when they have been in opposite directions for centuries in their "discerning and declaring the teaching of Scripture"?

These doctrinal points are so broad they're meaningless, especially contrasted to other irreconcilable theological difficulties. Nevertheless, according to *Catholics and Evangelicals Together*, these "difficulties must not be permitted to overshadow the truths on which we are, *by the grace of God, in firm agreement*" (ibid., 24, 25, italics supplied). And once in "agreement" doctrinally, they can unite politically. Indeed, once through the theological pablum, the document gets to its real concern.

"Christians individually and the church corporately also have a responsibility," it reads, "for the right ordering of civil society. . . . In the exercise of these public responsibilities there has been in recent years a growing convergence and cooperation between Evangelicals and Catholics. We thank God for the discovery of one another in contending for a common cause" (ibid., 12).

Putting aside rhetoric about the Holy Spirit leading Catholics and evangelicals into "all truth," the real focus of the document is abortion, "parental choice in education," a "vibrant market economy," religious freedom, pornography, family values, an "appreciation of Western culture," and "a realistic and responsible understanding of America's part in world affairs" (ibid., 12-19). And though those signing the document claim to believe in separation of church and state, they are "deeply concerned by the courts' narrowing of the protections provided by the 'free exercise' provision of the First Amendment and by an obsession with 'no establishment' that stifles the necessary role of religion in American life" (ibid., 14).

These are issues on which Catholics and evangelicals can cooperate. The document dedicates almost ten pages to moral and political agreements (more than twice the space dedicated to theological ones). Those signing the document are more in harmony on abortion than on Mary's role in salvation; their shared concern about pornography overshadows their differences regarding the pope's authority; and a common desire for "reason and religion in contending for the foundational truths of our constitutional order" (ibid., 13) outweighs their differences on "justification by grace."

"Roman Catholics and evangelical Protestants," wrote columnist William Murchison, "dropped a sledgehammer hint concerning the shape of the twenty-first century. They threw their arms around each other—figuratively at least—and said henceforth in these troublous times they want to stand together, small differences being less important than large similarities."[14] After all, why let "small differences"—such as what Christ did or did not accomplish at the cross or how a person is saved or who interprets the Bible—separate Catholics and Protestants when they have "large similarities" on the important Christian themes of an "appreciation of Western culture" and "parental choice in education"?

The goals of the document, said *Church and State* magazine,

> are identical to those long touted by the moral majoritarians of both the Protestant and Catholic Right. The signers want a religiously oriented public school system, a tax-funded parochial school system and a church-state wall so low that theocrats can leap across and impose their religious traditions on others at will. The manifesto is not so much an advance in interfaith dialogue as a thinly veiled political campaign, albeit one styled in fancy intellectual and theological trappings.
>
> In essence, document signers are agreeing to ignore (or

compromise) deep differences of religious belief in order to press ahead with an anti-separationist political agenda.[15]

Church and State, essentially, reiterates what Ellen White wrote about Catholics and Protestants uniting on such "points of doctrine as are held by them in common" so that they can "influence the state to enforce their decrees and to sustain their institutions"[16] or, as the recently signed document expressed it, contend "for the right ordering of civil society."

After sounding a tepid caution, *Christianity Today* said that "evangelicals should applaud this effort and rejoice in the progress it represents."[17]

"I really do think it is a historic moment," said John White, president of Geneva College and former president of the National Association of Evangelicals. "I don't know of any other time in history when these two communities have . . . spoken together."[18]

"After nearly four centuries of division and hostility," wrote James Wallis, Jr., "Protestants and Catholics have taken an important step toward unity. Forty key Evangelical and Catholic leaders signed a statement at the Institute of Religion and Public Life in New York City on March 29, 1994, urging their followers to accept each other as Christians, put aside differences and contend for common civil causes."[19]

The headline to an article in *Moody* magazine about the new relationship between Catholics and evangelicals sounded right out of *The Great Controversy*. It's called "Across the Divide."[20]

"This is the wave of the future," said Christian Coalition executive director Dr. Ralph Reed. "It is as significant a coalition to the future of American Politics as the unification of blacks and Jews during the civil rights struggle."[21]

Reed pulled away the veneer of religion and got to the core: "the future of American Politics." This document is not about the leading of the Holy Spirit or "full communion between Christians." It's about conservative Catholics and Protestants pooling their numbers, talents, and money in order to achieve a political agenda. If anything, religion has divided, not unified, Catholics and Protestants—and *Evangelicals and Catholics Together* attempts to get religion out of the way so they can concentrate on their "common civil causes."

"A generation ago," wrote Gustav Niebuhr in the *New York Times*, "such a grouping would have been highly unlikely, given the differences in understanding of the role of the Bible, tradition and ecclesiastical authority that divide Catholics from evangelicals. But times have changed."[22]

Have they really? Nineteen hundred years ago, rival factions of the same faith—Sadducees and Pharisees—put aside their theological differences in order to pursue a common political goal. Their immediate temporal concern—the fear that "the Romans shall come and take away both our place and nation" (John 11:48)—overshadowed their long historical hatred, and they united in opposing Christ.

With *Evangelicals and Catholics Together*, rival factions of the same faith—Protestants and Catholics—are putting aside their theological differences in order to pursue a common political goal. Their immediate temporal concern—"the common good"—has overshadowed their long historical hatred, and they are uniting against "all that opposes Christ and his cause"[23] and who are "enemies of the cause of Christ."[24]

For centuries each group claimed that members of the other were "opposed to Christ and His cause" or were "enemies of the cause of Christ," especially because of the theological differences that they now regard as the source of a "needless and loveless conflict" (ibid.) between them, differences that stand in the way of the "unity that Christ intends for all his disciples" (ibid., 2). They no longer regard each other as adversaries ("all who accept Christ as Lord and Savior are brothers and sisters in Christ") (ibid., 5); they have, apparently, saved that role for others instead.

"The time cometh," Jesus warned, "that whosoever killeth you will think that he doeth God service. And these things will they do unto you, because they have not known the Father, nor me. But these things have I told you, that when the time shall come, ye may remember that I told you of them" (John 16:2-4).

"Those who honor the Bible Sabbath will be denounced as enemies of law and order," wrote Ellen White, "as breaking down the moral restraints of society, causing anarchy and corruption, and calling down the judgments of God upon the earth. Their conscientious scruples will be pronounced obstinacy, stubbornness, and contempt of authority. They will be accused of disaffection toward the government. Ministers who deny the obligation of the divine law will present from the pulpit the duty of yielding obedience to the civil authorities as ordained of God. In legislative halls and courts of justice, commandment keepers will be misrepresented and condemned."[25]

Evangelicals and Catholics Together doesn't name the so-called "enemies of the cause of Christ."

But then again, it doesn't have to.

---

1. *Evangelicals and Catholics Together: The Christian Mission in the Third Millennium*, Final Draft, 29 March 1994.

2. Alister E. McGrath, "Do We Still Need the Reformation?" *Christianity Today*, 12 December 1994, 28.

3. *Evangelicals and Catholics Together*, 19.

4. Ibid., 1.

5. Quoted in Kenneth Kantzer, "A Most Misunderstood Woman," *Christianity Today*, 12 December 1986, 19.

6. *Evangelicals and Catholics Together*, 2.

7. H. Grattan Guinness, quoted in *Romanism and the Reformation* (London: 1891), 158.

8. Ibid., 159.

9. *Evangelicals and Catholics Together*, 4.

10. Ibid., 8.

11. Land and Lewis did, however, under incessant criticism from many constituents, have their names removed from the document, though they said that "we believe the document signifies a new era of cooperation on such concerns as freedom of religion, pornography, attack on faith and family and abortion. We therefore continue to disagree vigorously with uninformed and distorted criticism" (*Nashville Tennessean*, 5 April 1995).

12. *Evangelicals and Catholics Together*, 2.

13. Ibid., 5.

14. William Murchison, "What's Wrong With Fundamentalists Anyway?" *Conservative Chronicle*, 27 April 1994, 30.

15. "Religious Liberty and the 'Third Millennium': Rule of the Righteous," *Church and State*, May 1994, 11.

16. Ellen G. White, *The Great Controversy* (Boise, Idaho: Pacific Press Publishing Assn., 1950), 445.

17. Timothy George, "Catholics and Evangelicals in the Trenches," *Christianity Today*, 16.

18. Quoted in *Church and State*, May 1994, 8.

19. James R. Wallis, Jr., "Historic Christian Declaration Signed," *Christian American*, May/June 1994, 1.

20. Davis Duggins, "Across the Divide," *Moody*, November 1993, 12.

21. Quoted by James R. Wallis, *Christian American*, 1.

22. Gustav Niebuhr, "Forming Earthly Alliances to Defend God's Kingdom," *New York Times*, 28 August 1994.

23. *Evangelicals and Catholics Together*, 11.

24. Ibid., 4.

25. *The Great Controversy*, 592.

CHAPTER
TWO

"Jesus said that this would indicate that He was 'at the door,' ready to return. Then He said, 'Truly I say to you, *this generation* will not pass away until all these things take place' (Matthew 24:34, NASB). What generation? Obviously, in context, the generation that would see the signs—chief among them the rebirth of Israel. A generation in the Bible is something like forty years. If this is a correct deduction, then within forty years or so of 1948, all these things could take place. Many scholars who have studied Bible prophecy all their lives believe that this is so" (Hal Lindsey, *The Late Great Planet Earth*, 43).

"The prophecy of Daniel 9:27 tells us exactly what will start the tribulation period: when 'he [the prince that shall come] shall confirm a covenant with many of one week.' It seems that the Antichrist will make a covenant with Daniel's people for seven years" (Tim LaHaye, *How to Study Bible Prophecy for Yourself*, 67).

"The material set forth in this book has been done so with great care. Care was constantly exercised to make sure that no Biblical data was forced or 'fudged' to make it fit into a preconceived idea. Every attempt was made to be faithful to the Bible. The results of this study teach that the month of September of the year 1994 is to be the time for the end of history" (Harold Camping).

Two times in particular make me exceedingly thankful to be a Seventh-day Adventist. The first is when I'm in a restaurant, watching the masses dig their own graves, a mouthful at a time, with their teeth. Though far from a model health reformer (I like Häagen-Dazs too much), when I watch people gorge themselves on pork, beef, clams, and oysters, washing them down with beer, wine, and tequila, and then finish off by sucking tobacco smoke into their lungs—I thank God for the simple health message.

The second is whenever I either read or hear other conservative Christians expound on the last days.

Despite year after year of failed dates, millions continue to believe in the secret rapture. It's taught in religious colleges, expounded from pulpits, promulgated from mainline Christian bookstores, and preached on radio and television all over the world. John F. Walvoord, president and professor of Systematic Theology at Dallas Theological Seminary for more than a decade and the author or editor of twenty-seven books, wrote *Armageddon, Oil, and the Middle East Crisis* (published by the mammoth Christian publisher Zondervan) during the Gulf War. His book devoted a chapter to the rapture—a time when Christians will be secretly taken from the earth by Jesus and spared the tribulation of the end.

"It would be difficult," Walvoord wrote, "not to be troubled if Scripture did not clearly show that inevitable martyrdom in the Great Tribulation would not be the next expectation for believers in this age. True Christians today need not fear the catastrophic days about to overcome the world. Instead, they have the imminent hope of Christ's return and their being joined to the Lord to enjoy His presence forever."[1]

For millions of our Bible-believing Christian brothers and sisters, the Middle East, particularly Israel, remains at the forefront of last-day events. From tongue-speaking charismatics in California to Baptist fundamentalists in Alabama, the central focus of eschatology deals not with papal Rome or the United States, but with the Jews. Almost any evangelical or fundamentalist bookstore overflows with books—published by reputable Christian presses— that focus on the Middle East as the center of prophetic events. One magazine article links the signing of the Israeli-PLO peace accord in 1993 *with Daniel 9:24-27*, particularly the section about confirming "the covenant with many for one week" (Daniel 9:26).

"The September 13 agreement signed by Israel and the PLO does deal with the status of Jerusalem," the article says, "and does confirm the Jerusalem covenant." Therefore,

> if the Antichrist was in attendance at the signing of the Arab-Israeli agreement on September 13, 1993, then we are almost certainly in the final seven years to Armageddon right now! If he

was not, it appears that he must appear on the world scene very quickly to confirm the covenant. Whichever is true, we know that we do live in the time of the most dramatic prophetic fulfillments in the history of the world![2]

Almost all conservative Christians still await the antichrist. Despite the clear testimony of the Bible, the Protestant Reformers, and centuries of Protestant history, almost all conservative Christian—with few exceptions—have turned away from papal Rome to a soon-to-be-revealed power. Historian Paul Boyer wrote that "the Vatican faded after 1945 as a target of Antichrist watchers."[3] Instead, a police line-up of potential antichrists have arisen, everyone from Henry Kissinger, Kurt Waldheim, Sun Myung Moon, Anwar el-Sadat, and King Juan Carlos of Spain. In the late 1980s, a book called *Gorbachev! Has the Real Antichrist Come?*, by Robert Faid, noted that in Russian, the numerical equivalent of "Mikhail S. Gorbachev" was 1,332, or 666 x 2.[4] Pat Robertson has even speculated at the antichrist's age: "If the antichrist is yet to come, then we must conclude that there is a man alive today, approximately twenty-seven years old, who is being groomed to be the Satanic messiah."[5]

In 1983, Detroit lawyer Constance Cumbey wrote a number-one bestseller, *The Hidden Dangers of the Rainbow*, which warned that the New Age movement was the antichrist power (at least Cumbey correctly identified it as a *power* rather than as an individual).

"Clearly," Cumbey wrote, "if we have such a movement that meets the biblical specifications of the antichrist, existing simultaneously in history with the fulfillment of other end-time prophecies such as those regarding the restoration of Israel, then Christians and indeed not just Christians, but all who seek the truth and have concerns for our future, should take a very careful look at that Movement."[6]

The prevalency of these speculations proves that most Christians don't know one of the most fundamental and important truths regarding last-day events, the identity of the beast powers in Revelation 13 and 14.

For years, too, mainline Christian bookstores have sold books, tracts, and tapes outlining the Soviet Union's role as Ezekiel's infamous Gog. "It seems almost certain," wrote Jerry Falwell, "that Ezekiel refers to none other than the Red Communist Bear, the

U.S.S.R."[7] Wrote Robertson: "The Soviet Union is going to make a move against this little nation known as Israel. And that's going to happen because it's very clear-cut in the Bible in the last days."[8]

Apparently, it wasn't as clear-cut as Robertson thought, especially since the Soviet Union is gone, and along with it the basic prophetic scenario that millions of fundamentalist Christians held for decades.

However, much of the Soviet empire's collapse didn't fit into *their* last-day events scenario; it fit into *ours*—perfectly. Though the demise of the "Red Communist Bear" has forced the evangelicals to rewrite their prophetic books, it has made ours more pertinent than ever.

With all the dizzying prophetic speculations and date setting of evangelical Protestantism, the three angels' messages of Revelation 13 sit like a rock amid the storm blowing these Christians to one ridiculous reinterpretation after another, one failed prophetic scenario after another, one failed date after another. We Adventists have our kooks and date setters as well, and they seem to be on the rise, but they don't represent mainline Adventism, which for years has firmly, steadfastly (with few exceptions) held a steady course, adhering to Bible- and Spirit of Prophecy–based teaching that, in the face of recent events, more than ever validate our message.

Of course, we still have scoffers. Recently, an Adventist speaking to an audience of ministers subtly (he had to be subtle; he was a denominational employee) mocked our prophetic message. He talked about some Adventists (definitely not mainstream) who, linking the Vietnam War with Revelation's "kings of the east," saw that conflict as a harbinger of the end. Then, in the same breath, he ridiculed those Adventists who see the collapse of the Soviet Union as a sign of the end, too, thus linking both views and making the latter look as stupid as the former. While only a fool would link the Vietnam War with Revelation's "kings of the east," only a bigger one could not see the Soviet Union's fall as a major step toward the fulfillment of prophecy. As I listened, one truth struck me with resounding clarity: whenever Seventh-day Adventists are hung from lampposts because of the Sabbath, some among us—even those of stature and influence—will still scoff at our beliefs.

Nevertheless, even with all the reasons we have to believe our prophetic scenario, questions remain, even hard ones. And one of the hardest deals with America's prophetic role. Even as events unfold (such as the signing of *Evangelicals and Catholics Together*), how could the United States ever be, as Ellen White warned, the last power "that is to wage war against the church and the law of God"?[9] How could this nation—which taught the world the principles of religious freedom—turn into the oppressive regime that "spake as a dragon" (Revelation 13:11) and forces "as many as would not worship the image of the beast [to] be killed" (verse 15)?

More than two hundred years after its founding, the United States still allows freedoms that men and women never even dared dream of during most of history. The wall of separation of church and state—the key to this freedom—still stands high and firm. In 1994, for example, the U.S. Supreme Court, in *Kiryas Joel*, upheld a lower-court decision that ruled that a special school district established to accommodate the needs of handicapped children of Satmar Hasidim (orthodox Jews) was an unconstitutional violation of the Establishment Clause. How would this nation, which—out of fear of violating the Establishment Clause—forbid a tiny orthodox Jewish sect from having a special school district to accommodate handicapped children, kill those who don't keep Sunday as a holy day?

We don't know. We haven't been told, exactly. But one point remains certain: the change could happen easier, and faster, than anyone could imagine.

Most born and bred Americans accept our religious rights as natural to our existence as our food, water, and shelter. Yet the American experiment in freedom—and that's what it has always been, an experiment—is the exception to the rule, which is that for almost all human history, the masses have lived without the freedoms that we assume are birthrights.

"We hold these truths to be self-evident," said the Declaration of Independence, "that all men are created equal, that they are endowed by their Creator with certain unalienable Rights, that among these are Life, Liberty and the pursuit of Happiness."[10] Yet how "self-evident" are these truths, if out of six thousand years of human history, only in the past two hundred has any nation ever seriously attempted to base its laws upon them? How self-evident could they be when Thomas Jefferson, who penned those words, and many of the men who signed them—owned slaves? Every one of these "self-evident" truths and the freedoms derived from them had to be unearthed like small precious gems from the centuries-high trash heap of human carnage and waste caused by despotism, apostasy, and dogma. Each freedom has been established only with blood, sweat, and tears—and only with blood, sweat, and tears can they remain. And yet even then they will still be lost!

"In our land of boasted freedom," warned the prophet, "religious liberty will come to an end."[11]

Many of our freedoms, which we assume are chiseled into the granite foundation of the constitutional American republic, are really just lightly penciled across the surface. It wouldn't take much to remove, cover, or change them. They have always been tampered with; there have always been those who want to erase them; and, according to prophecy, they will succeed.

In times of crisis, basic rights, even in the land of the free, have been treated as if they were written by a finger across the dusty back window of a pickup truck rather than in the U.S. Constitution. Numerous times the government has taken prerogatives that resulted in the violation of constitutional rights, often with the courts—the supposed protector of these rights—rolling over and playing dead.

For example, despite all the promises in the Bill of Rights about the due process of law—which is supposed to guarantee that no one is arrested or imprisoned without all the protections afforded to citizens by the law—thousands of American men, women, and children were uprooted from their homes and put in prison camps for years, even though they violated no laws, were charged with no crimes, and were given no trials. All this, long after the Constitution had forbade this type of infringement of rights.

How did it happen? Americans became scared, and their fears took precedence over firmly established constitutional principles. It happened before, it can happen again, and—if we believe our prophetic message—it *will* happen again, only worse.

If, in a crisis, this nation could ignore rights clearly written in the Constitution, how easily in another crisis it could enforce a strict Sunday law, especially when nothing in the document expressly forbids Sunday legislation. Actually, the Constitution itself acknowledges Sunday, and the U.S. Supreme Court has already upheld the constitutionality of Sunday laws.

What's even worse is that part of the Court's rationale for Sunday legislation has been that James Madison, the man who wrote the First Amendment, also introduced into the Virginia legislature "A Bill for Punishing the Disturbers of Religious Worship and Sabbath Breakers."[12] When we have James Madison, the architect of religious freedom in America, promoting a Sunday law—we have problems!

We have more than we think. However much we might assume the contrary, history, jurisprudence, and the Constitution don't necessarily work in favor of our traditional positions. Sunday might be the "pope's Sabbath," "the false Sabbath," the upcoming sign of "the mark of the beast," but it has a long tradition in this nation that many Americans haven't forgotten and that the courts have upheld.

Despite propaganda about the imminence of Sunday laws, there isn't much support for them now. Yet under circumstances not that hard to imagine, a Sunday law would be easy to pass.

This book will explore, among other things, how easy. It will look at the most recent attacks on religious liberty in light of our understanding of last-day events. It will show the reasoning, logic, and validity of arguments opposed to our positions. Adventists will be surprised at how flimsy is the foundation of the freedoms that we take for granted. Many of our rights are not specifically written in the Constitution itself, but have been the creation of the Court, which has at times used faulty logic, reasoning, and history to establish those rights. The book will show, too, that, in the final crisis, our defense can't be in the Constitution, in the courts, or in what the Founding Fathers said and did, because the Constitution, the courts, and the Founding Fathers don't always harmonize with our positions.

What, then, can we trust?

Read on and find out.

---

1. John F. Walvoord, *Armageddon, Oil, and the Middle East Crisis* (Grand Rapids, Mich.: Zondervan, 1990), 205.

2. Irvin Baxter, Jr., "Seven Years to Armageddon: Is the Israeli-PLO Agreement the Beginning of the Final Seven Years?" *Endtime*, Special Edition, 1993, 20.

3. Paul Boyer, *When Time Shall Be No More* (Cambridge: Harvard University Press, 1992), 275.

4. Ibid., 178.

5. Quoted in William Alnor, *Soothsayers of the Second Advent* (Old Tappan, N.J.: Fleming Revell, 1989), 25.

6. Constance Cumbey, *The Hidden Dangers of the Rainbow* (Shreveport, La.: Huntington House, 1983), 42.

7. Quoted in Clifford Goldstein, "What Ever Happened to Gog?" *Liberty*, July 1992, 19.

8. Quoted in Ibid., 19.

9. Ellen G. White, "The Dragon Voice," *Signs of the Times*, 10 February 1910, 4.

10. "Consider what is probably the most famous single sentence ever written in the Western hemisphere. 'We hold these truths to be self-evident. . .' Immediately we notice that what seemed self-

evident to Thomas Jefferson would appear either patently false or meaningless or superstitious to most great men who keep shaping our civilization: to Aristotle, Machiavelli, Hobbes, Marx and all his followers, Nietzsche, Weber, and for that matter, to most contemporary political theorists" (Lesek Kolawski, Annual Jefferson Lecture, Washington, D.C., 1986).

11. Ellen G. White, *Evangelism* (Hagerstown, Md.: Review and Herald Publishing Assn., 1946), 326.

12. Report of the Committee of Revisors Appointed to the General Assembly of Virginia, MDCCLXXVI.

CHAPTER
THREE

"Just like what Nazi Germany did to the Jews, so liberal America is now doing to the evangelical Christians" (Pat Robertson, "Demagoguery in America," *The New Republic*, 1 August 1994, 1).

"Between 450 and 500 persons were crowded in a chamber measuring 125 square feet in Treblinka. Parents carried their children in the vain hope of saving them from death. On the way to their doom they were pushed and beaten with rifle butts and gas pipes. Dogs were set on them, barking, biting and tearing them. It lasted a short while. Then the doors were shut tightly with a bang. Twenty-five minutes later everybody was dead and they stood lifeless; there being no free space, they just leaned against each other" (Yankel Wiernik, Holocaust survivor).

More than a century ago, Ellen White warned that "the union of the church with the state, be the degree never so slight, while it may appears to bring the world nearer to the church, does in reality but bring the church nearer to the world."[1] The truth of her words appear in the New Christian Right, which increasingly resorts to the demagoguery typical of politicians and political parties, not Christians. Recently, to raise funds, increase membership, and attain power, the New Right has been convincing Christians in America that they—*are victims of religious persecution!*

Juxtaposing a picture of the fallen Berlin Wall with one of an abortion protestor being arrested, an advertisement by Pat Robertson's American Center for Law and Justice (ACLJ) asks, "Have we won the cold war . . . only to lose our own freedom?"

Jerry Falwell warns that "Bible-believing Christianity" has been "outlawed" in America.[2]

Pat Buchanan bemoans the "Christian-bashing" so prevalent in America today.[3]

William Bennett reports that it's "open season" on Christians.[4]

Tim LaHaye warns about "the government-inspired religious persecution that is going on in America today in the name of the first Amendment."[5]

The Rutherford Institute writes about "religious apartheid" against Christians.[6]

Charles Colson says that Christians have become a "persecuted minority."[7]

Even James Dobson has warned: "I believe that Christian oppression is just around the corner. I really believe that the level of anger rising out of the homosexual community primarily, but the whole humanistic movement that's out there . . . as they gain political power—and they got it now—they're going to continue to oppress us."[8]

New Right lawyer Keith Fournier explains: "Day after day, the news media brings us horrific reports from the Balkans, Africa, and other foreign countries of ethnic-based attacks all-too reminiscent of the infamous Holocaust. . . . And yet, a similar insanity is being perpetrated before our eyes in our own country. But ethnic origin isn't the target. It's religion and those who embrace it."[9]

What indignities—reminiscent of the Balkan and African carnage—do "those who embrace" religion (i.e., conservative Christians) face in America today?

Hollywood doesn't portray Christians nicely. The media says mean things about them. They can't display religious symbols on government property. Representative Vic Fabio and President Bill Clinton have criticized their political activities. They can't get government money to fund parochial education. They're not allowed to teach creationism in public schools. The *New York Times* doesn't count Christian books on its bestseller list. Christians are stopped from instituting public prayer at graduation ceremonies. And, in warning about the greatest threat to Christians since Nero used them for street lamps, an ACLJ tract said that "a standup comic relates a tasteless joke about evangelists, as the talk show host guffaws his approval."

How, for example, does media mogul Pat Robertson—founder and chairman of Christian Broadcasting Network; founder and chairman of U.S. Media Corp.; founder and chairman of International

Family Entertainment, Inc.; chairman of NorthStar Entertainment; founder and president of the Christian Coalition; founder and president of the American Center for Law and Justice; chairman of the Broadcast Equities, Inc.; host of the 700 Club; founder of Operation Blessing; founder and chancellor of Regent's University; and presidential candidate—find courage to survive amidst an environment as hostile to Christians as Nazi Europe was to the Jews?

Such commitment, for example, makes the sufferings of Richard Wurmbrand, who spent fourteen years in Communist prisons, seem benign. "Christians were hung," he wrote, "upside down on ropes and beaten so severely that their bodies swung back and forth under the blows. Christians were put in ice-box 'refrigerator cells' which were so cold, frost and ice covered the inside. I was thrown into one with very little clothing on. Prison doctors would watch through an opening until they saw the symptoms of freezing to death, then they would give a warning and guards would rush in to take us out and make us warm. When we were finally warmed, we would immediately be put back in the ice-box cells to freeze—over and over again. . . . Even today sometimes I can't bear to open a refrigerator."[10]

What would Christian martyrs—those fed to lions, burned at the stake, buried alive, beaten to death, shot, exiled, and imprisoned—think about the persecution of Christians in America today?

How much sympathy would poor American Christians receive from Christian martyr John Hooper? "The third fire was kindled within a while after, which was more extreme than the other two. In this fire he [Hooper] prayed with a loud voice, 'Lord Jesus, have mercy upon me! Lord Jesus receive my spirit!' These were the last words he was heard to utter. But when he was black in the mouth, and his tongue was so swollen that he could not speak, yet his lips went until they were shrunk to the gums: and he knocked his breast with his hands until one of his arms fell off."[11]

Or from the Huguenots in France after the revocation of the Edict of Nantes? "They hanged both men and women by their hair or their feet, and smoked them with hay until they were nearly dead; and if they still refused to sign a recantation, they hung them up again and repeated their barbarities. . . . Sometimes they tied fathers and husbands, while they ravished their wives and daughters before their eyes. Multitudes they imprisoned in the most noisome dungeons, where they practised all sorts of torments in secret."[12]

How would the apostle Paul—eventually to face martyrdom him-self—view the whining, especially as he (from a Roman prison!) could write: "I count all things but loss for the excellency of the knowledge of Christ Jesus my Lord: for whom I have suffered the loss of all things, and do count them but dung" (Philippians 3:8).

How did the poor, suffering, outlawed Christians in 1994 pres-sure the U.S. House and Senate into voting, overwhelmingly, against EEOC religious harassment guidelines that they feared might be hostile to religion? Some persecuted minority!

Every Sunday, Christians of every stripe and hue file into churches situated on millions of dollars worth of land that the "hos-tile" government lets them own tax free. From their printing presses and publishing houses; from their radio and TV stations; from their schools, colleges, and seminaries; from their books, tracts, and maga-zines—Christians have not only been able to promote their reli-gious views, but the "anti-Christian" government has even made laws to ensure that they are not discriminated against because of those views.

Of course, some bias against Christianity does exist in America. But bias isn't persecution, any more than a Jewish joke is the Holocaust—and for these Christians to portray themselves as vic-tims of persecution makes a mockery of those Christians in other lands who truly are.

"Some conservative Christian activists," wrote Stephen Bates of the Annenberg Washington Program, "deem the victimization trend unscriptural. They note that the Bible tells Christians to expect persecution. 'The Apostle Paul would have never done such a thing,' one activist says of the victimization rhetoric. 'When the whole early church was being fed to the lions, they weren't whining.'"[13]

"I am honestly bewildered," wrote Michael Kinsley in the *New Republic*, "by the frequent complaint that American culture is hos-tile to religion—that religious beliefs are routinely belittled and held up to scorn. That has been a familiar theme of conservatives and neocons over recent years. And it is the burden of *The Culture of Disbelief* (Basic Books), an interesting new book by Yale Law professor Stephen Carter, a liberal. . . . What on earth are these people talking about? To be sure, the Supreme Court has made a mess of the Constitution's anathema on the 'Establishment' of reli-gion, and officials sometimes get carried away in protecting the secularism of public institutions. But are 'Americans [who] take their religion seriously' consigned 'to the lunatic fringe,' as Carter would have it? Is there a 'steady drumbeat' in American culture 'that the religiously devout are less rational than more "normal" folks'? Are those who 'pray regularly' forced to keep it a 'shameful secret'? Not in any America I recognize."[14]

To pawn off Christians in America as victims of persecution similar to what the Jews suffered under the Nazis or what Muslim minorities are suffering in the Balkans reveals just how corrupted the New Christian Right has become. Lies and exaggerations are tools of the world, not the church, unless, of course, the church becomes part of the world. As Ellen White warned, once church and state start uniting, it's the church that becomes like the state, not vice versa. How ironic, because the Christian Right's involvement in politics is, ostensibly, to turn the nation to God; instead, the nation is turning the Christian Right away from Him. And, the more political the New Christian Right becomes, the farther away it will go.

"Whatever the position adopted by the church," wrote historian-philosopher Jacques Ellul, "every time she becomes involved in politics, on every occasion the result is unfaithfulness to herself and the abandonment of the truths of the gospel. . . . Every time the church has played the power game . . . she has been misled to act treasonably, either toward truth or incarnate love."[15]

Though the New Right often portrays its struggle as spiritual—Christ against Satan, light against darkness, truth against error—it's really engaged in a worldly battle using worldly methods. Running stealth candidates (people who seek election to office while hiding their ties to the New Right), taking over party caucuses, forming political alliances, mudslinging—all of which the New Right does—might be part of the political process, but it shouldn't be confused with the gospel. However, as the New Right has apparently learned, it's easier to write laws in statute books than on hearts, which is why it is more preoccupied with winning elections than souls.

"We think," said Ralph Reed, "the Lord is going to give us this nation back one precinct at a time, one neighborhood at a time and one state at a time."[16] If that's how "the Lord" is going to give the "nation back" to them, He certainly hasn't revealed these methods in Scripture.

"I do guerrilla warfare," said Reed. "I paint my face invisible and travel at night. You don't know it's over until you're in a body bag. You don't know until election night." That might be good politics, but what has it to do with Jesus and the gospel?

"Secular revolutions," wrote Ellul, "in reality do not essentially revolutionize the world at all. They use the methods of the world to change the world. They operate with the basic framework of sinful civilization. Thus utilizing what this world itself offers them, they become its slaves."[17]

The power that Christians should seek comes, as Ellen White wrote, "not by the decisions of courts or councils or legislative assemblies, ... but by the implanting of Christ's nature in humanity through the work of the Holy Spirit. ... Now, as in Christ's day, the work of God's kingdom lies not with those who are clamoring for recognition and support by earthly rulers and human laws."[18] However, if devoid of power from above, you have to seek it elsewhere, exactly what the Christian Right is doing.

"The kingdom of Christ," wrote evangelical Michael Horton, "is not advanced by the legislation of ideology but by the proclamation of theology, namely, the gospel of God's grace in Christ. When moralism replaces confidence in the saving work of Christ, the church not only fails to transform the moral life of the culture, it actually serves the process of secularization by leaving its central affirmations and settling for the moral victories of paganism when the greater spiritual victory of Christianity appears to them beyond reach."[19]

Of course, only by the complete corruption of the church can prophecy be fulfilled. A spirit-filled, Christ-centered church won't turn the lamblike beast of Revelation 13 into one that speaks as a dragon. A church connected to Christ and fulfilling the gospel commission isn't going to seek economic sanctions against those who don't "worship the beast."

In contrast, a corrupted "clergy will put forth almost superhuman efforts to shut away the light lest it should shine upon their flocks."[20] A church converted to the world, not to Christ, will appeal "to the strong arm of civil power" to enforce its dogmas. A weak, compromised Christianity will urge "that the few who stand in opposition to an institution of the church and a law of the state ought not to be tolerated; that it is better for them to suffer than for whole nations to be thrown into confusion and lawlessness."[21] Only an apostate worldly church that has political control—exactly what the New Christian Right is becoming—will fulfill prophecy.

"If Christian people work together," said Pat Robertson, "they can succeed in winning back control of the institutions that have been taken from them over the past 70 years. Expect confrontations that will be not only unpleasant but bloody. . . . This decade will not be for the faint of heart, but the resolute. Institutions will be plunged into wrenching change. We will be living through one of the most tumultuous periods in human history. When it is over I am convinced that God's people will emerge victorious. But no victory ever comes without a battle."[22]

A "bloody" battle for political control? Was Robertson intimating violence? These are the words of a politician, not of a Christian—not even of a Christian politician. Again, is the New Right changing the state, or is the state changing the New Right?

However ridiculous the claim that Christians are victims of persecution in America, the concept is a stroke of political (if not spiritual) genius. "It is hard to make a case that evangelical Christians are being systematically victimized," wrote Tim Stafford of *Christianity Today*. "They look too robustly middle class for that."[23] Yet that is exactly the case the New Right is making, and with apparent success, too, because the movement has been growing as never before.

What better way to shake evangelicals out of their political complacency than to convince them that they are victims? If evangelicals can be persuaded that the wall of separation of church and state is persecuting them, that laws forbidding government-sponsored prayer in school are persecuting them, that the arrest of abortion protestors is persecuting them, and that movies like *The Last Temptation of Christ* are persecuting them, they will respond. They already are.

"Reveille has sounded in America," began a cover article in *The Palm Beach Post*, "and conservative Christians are rising from the pews and heading for the precincts, striving to build an alliance between God and government. . . . They're becoming active in the schools, on library boards, in city halls, state capitols and the Republican Party. They're changing attitudes—and laws."[24]

"We've seen a lot in our history," said political scientist John Green about the growing power of the Religious Right, "but I don't know that America has ever seen anything like this."[25]

"The religious conservatives," wrote Irving Kristol in the *Wall*

Street Journal, "are already too numerous to be shunted aside, and their numbers are growing, as is their influence. They are going to be the very core of an emerging American conservatism. . . . Today it is the religious who have a sense that the tide has turned and that the wave of the future is moving in their direction."[26]

"For the religious right," wrote Sidney Blumenthal in *The New Yorker,* "invisibility is no longer possible. From South Carolina to Oregon, state parties are falling under its sway. . . . Across the nation, the flag and the cross are becoming one."[27]

I remember years ago talking to a charismatic girl involved in the Religious Right. She said that she had been skeptical about getting into politics but changed her mind after reading that the American government was out to persecute Christians. Therefore, she had to fight back.

"You know, Cliff," she said, "the government wants to take our Bibles from us."

Take our Bibles from us?

I don't blame the girl; I blame the demagogues who under the veil of Christianity are deceiving the flock into the belief that they are persecuted.

Recently a Christian magazine had a picture of a man dressed in a Nazi uniform stomping on a cross; on the opposite page it warned that "we must raise up the cross from under the oppressor's feet. We must fight the good fight. We must take a stand and find a voice and stay true to the principles that constitute our faith. We shall overcome."[28]

If Christians need to "raise up the cross" from under the oppressor's feet, they must, of course, identify the oppressors, or those whom *Evangelicals and Catholic Together* describes as "enemies of Christ and his cause." This ploy worked for the Nazis: portray the righteous German *volk* as persecuted and oppressed, and then identify the persecutors and the oppressors. The New Christian Right is doing the same. It's moved from the Cold War, in which the enemy was the Soviet Union—to the Culture War, in which enemy includes the ACLU, liberals, secular humanists, and homosexuals, among others. No doubt many of these people and groups represent views that any Christian, New Right or not, would find abhorrent. Yet for those who profess the name of Christ to label them as enemies and persecutors might be good politics, but, again, what has that to do with the meek and gentle Jesus?

"What is so disturbing," wrote Mike Yaconelli, "is what fear is doing to the right-wing, conservative church in America. They, like all of us, are afraid of the disintegration of our society. They, like all of us, are concerned about the increasing violence, the hatred and anger that rule our cities, the collapse of the family, and the moral vertigo that characterizes our leaders.

"What worries me is not our common fear, it is what is happening to the conservative, fundamental wing of the Church in the face of that fear: they are sending, with their blessing, an army of religious bounty hunters to label and destroy anyone they consider an enemy. The bounty hunters are allowed to roam freely on the pages of Christian books and on the airwaves of Christian radio and television, pointing their fingers at anyone they consider to be the enemy."[29]

"I want you to let a wave of intolerance wash over you," said activist Randall Terry. "I want you to let a wave of hatred wash over you. Yes, hate is good. . . . Our goal is a Christian nation. We have a biblical duty, we are called by God, to conquer this country."[30]

Quoting Winston Churchill, an ACLJ tract said: "Victory at all costs, victory in spite of all terror, victory however long and hard the road may be; for without victory there is no survival." It then says that "the religious and civil liberties fought for by the Founding Fathers may not last for our children. Unless we take action now."[31]

The rhetoric sounds as if the authors were Christians in Nero's Rome, not evangelicals living in a nation that allows them the freedom they would use to destroy freedom for others. In an article for *Liberty*, Albert Menendez and Edd Doerr, two church-state experts, showed just how wealthy, prosperous, and influential Christians are in this country, exposing the nonsense about Christian persecution in America. According to the article, 93 percent of the 104th Congress claims to be Christian; evangelical booksellers did one billion dollars of business in 1994; clergy still rank high in American minds for ethical standards (even after Swaggert and Bakker); contributions among the forty-four largest Protestant churches in 1992 were more than sixteen billion; and top government officials often link religion to secular power. Hardly the stuff that persecution is made of.

"The facts are irrefutable," they wrote. "If any systematic 'attempt to drive Christians and the Christian faith into oblivion' exists, it isn't doing so well. The 'club' of church-state separation hasn't battered the Christian enterprise in America too badly. Religion in America, especially evangelical Christianity, seems to be holding its own in the areas of membership, finance, and political influence. If this is persecution, church leaders ought to be praying for more."[32]

The truth is that, despite the rhetoric, no nation in history has given people the freedoms that Christians still enjoy in America. Even William Bennett, though bemoaning the "open season" on Christians, recently wrote that "we Americans have achieved unprecedented prosperity and freedom."[33] He's right, but that fact won't raise money, gain recruits, and amass power for the New Christian Right, which is why—despite its truth—the New Right will never say it. Instead, the New Right will continue down its political road, continually being corrupted by the system it claims that God has called it to purify.

Paul's words that "all that will live godly in Christ Jesus shall suffer persecution" (2 Timothy 3:12) prove why—despite their whining—these people haven't been persecuted at all.

---

1. *The Great Controversy*, 297.
2. Quoted in Stephen Bates, "Political Christians: The Bully Pulpit Meets the Lions' Den," *Washington Post*, 17 July 1994, C3.
3. Pat Buchanan, "What's the Christian-bashing All About?" *Conservative Chronicle*, 29 June 1994, 21.
4. Quoted in Colman McCarthy, "The Religious Right's Slant on Christianity," *Liberal Opinion*, 18 July 1994, 1.
5. Tim LaHaye, *Faith of Our Founding Fathers* (Brentwood, Tenn.: Wolgemuth & Hyatt, 1987), 13.
6. Sheila McThenia, "Religious Apartheid," *Rutherford*, June 1994, 5.
7. Charles Colson, "From a Moral Majority to a Persecuted Minority," *Christianity Today*, 80.
8. Quoted in *The Journal of Church and State* 36, no. 2, 446.
9. Keith Fournier, *Religious Cleansing in the American Republic* (Washington, D.C.: Life, Liberty, and Family Publications, 1993), 4.
10. Richard Wurmbrand, *Tortured for Christ* (Glendale, Calif.: Diane Books, 1969), 36, 37.
11. *Fox's Book of Martyr's* (New York: Holt, Reinhart, and Winston, 1954), 215.
12. Ibid., 54.
13. Quoted in Stephan Bates, "Political Christians: The Bully Pulpit Meets the Lions' Den," C4.
14. Michael Kinsley, "Martyr Complex," *The New Republic*, 13 September 1993, 4.
15. Jacques Ellul, *Fausse Presense Au Monde*, 105-111. Quoted in *The Best of Hegstad* (Silver Spring, Md.: Department of Public Affairs and Religious Liberty, 1994), 6.
16. Ralph Reed, *Religious News Service*, 1 May 1994. Quoted in *The Religious Right: The Assault on Tolerance and Pluralism in America* (New York: Anti-Defamation League, 1994), 5.
17. Quoted in Stephen Bates, "Political Christians: The Bully Pulpit Meets the Lions' Den," C4.
18. Ellen G. White, *The Desire of Ages* (Boise, Idaho: Pacific Press Publishing Assn., 1940), 509, 510.
19. Michael Scott Horton, ed., *Power Religion* (Chicago: Moody Press, 1992), 16.
20. *The Great Controversy*, 607.
21. Ibid., 615.

22. Quoted in op. cit. 15.
23. Tim Stafford, "Move Over, ACLU," *Christianity Today*, 25 October 1994, 22.
24. Candy Hatcher, "God Says to Take a Stand," *Palm Beach Post*, 12 December 1993, A1.
25. Quoted in John Gravois, "The New Holy War," *Houston Post*, 3 July 1994, A1.
26. Irving Kristol, "The Coming 'Conservative Century,' " *Wall Street Journal*, 1 February 1993.
27. Sidney Blumenthal, "Christian Soldiers," *The New Yorker*, 18 July 1994, 31, 32.
28. "Religious Apartheid," *Rutherford* Magazine, August 1994, 2, 3.
29. Mike Yaconelli, "Religious Bounty Hunters," *The Back Door*, June 1994, 36.
30. Quoted in op. cit. 16.
31. From ACLJ (American Center for Law and Justice) promotional tract, 1992.
32. Edd Doerr and Albert J. Menendez, "Persecution Complex," *Liberty*, March 1995, 17.
33. William J. Bennett, undated newsletter accompanying his *Index of Leading Cultural Indicators*, The Heritage Foundation, 1994.

CHAPTER FOUR

"We must use the doctrine of religious liberty to gain independence for Christian schools until we train up a generation of people who know that there is no religious neutrality. . . . Then they will get busy in constructing a Bible-based social, political, and religious order which finally denies the religious liberty of the enemies of God" (Christian author Gary North, quoted in *The Religious Right: The Assault on Tolerance and Pluralism in America*, 5, 6).

"If we will not be constrained from within by the power of God, we must be constrained from without by the power of the State, acting as God's agent" (Columnist Cal Thomas, *Harper's Magazine*, March 1995, 30).

In a blue-and-yellow shuttle bus heading to an airport one hot Texas Sunday, I sat across from a young couple. Both were carrying Bibles, and both looked as Southern Baptist as I do Jewish. I started a conversation and, when the woman said her husband was a lawyer, I mentioned that I edited a church-state separation magazine.

"Church-state separation?" He scowled.

"Yeah, religious freedom and all that," I responded.

"Shouldn't I have the religious freedom," he said, "to enforce my beliefs on others?"

"Well, that's interesting," I answered, "but what about the religious freedom of those who don't want your beliefs enforced on them?"

He scowled again, and the conversation ended.

This exchange, however trivial, symbolizes a change in conservative American Christianity that can have prophetic implications: the church's new distrust, if not unabashed hostility, to church-state separation.

Though a recent *U.S. News and World Report* poll showed that 53 percent of Americans believe that "church and state must remain 'completely separate' "[1] (an absurd question because church and state can—and should—never be "completely separate"), church-state separation is deemed by more and more conservative Christians as both un-American and antichristian.

Pat Robertson, a signer of *Evangelicals and Catholics Together*—which "strongly affirm[s] the separation of church and state"—has publicly attacked it elsewhere. Addressing four thousand attendees at a Christian Coalition rally in South Carolina, Pat Robertson derided the "radical left," saying—before a standing ovation—that "they have kept us in submission because they have talked about separation of church and state. There is no such thing in the Constitution. It's a lie of the left, and we're not going to take it anymore."[2]

A popular book among the New Christian Right, *The Myth of Separation,* by David Barton, asks on the back cover: "Did you know separation of church and state is a myth?"[3]

"The separation of church and state is," said David S. Nelson, director of Pat Robertson's Christian Coalition in Colorado, "(1) not a teaching of the founding fathers; (2) not an historical teaching; (3) not a teaching of law (except in recent years); not a biblical teaching. In summary, there should be absolutely no 'separation of church and state' in America."[4]

"The separation of church and state," said Robert Simonds of Citizens for Excellence in Education (CEE), "is a socialist myth perpetrated by the ACLU."[5]

"Our purpose must be to spread the gospel on the new mission field that the Lord has opened—public high schools," wrote attorney Jay Sekulow, a lawyer for the American Center for Law and Justice. "Yes, the so-called 'wall of separation' between church and state has begun to crumble."[6]

David Muralt, CEE director in Texas, said that separation of church and state is a "heathen idea. It's totally alien to the foundation of our country. We were a Christian society."[7]

"The Religious Right's war against separation of church and state," warned Rob Boston of Americans United, "has had damaging effects. Thanks to a steady torrent of anti-separationist propaganda from the Religious Right, millions of Americans now believe that leaders like James Madison and Thomas Jefferson didn't really support separation of church and state; that the separation concept was invented by Communists; that separation is hostile to religion; that the Supreme Court has been stacked with atheists determined to drive religion out of American life."[8]

Perhaps the most frightening shift has occurred among Southern Baptists, the largest Protestant denomination in the United States. After years of struggles, the fundamentalists won control of the church's governing body, the Southern Baptist Convention, and have radically deviated from the church's historic position on church-state separation. Instead, the leaders have not only cozied up to the New Right politically, but are adopting the New Right's stance on church-state separation. The fundamentalists "have committed themselves to a partisan strategy of collusion between church and state," wrote Baptist Bill Moyers, "that also makes a mockery of the historic Baptist principles of religious liberty."[9]

It was a Southern Baptist leader who ten years ago called the notion of the separation of church and state a figment of some infidel's imagination.

Though most Southern Baptist leaders have more tact, they have shifted the denomination to a position that could severely weaken the principles of church-state separation.

"Every church historian worth his tenure," wrote Baptist professor William R. Estep, "knows that Baptists from their earliest inception called for the institutional separation of church and state. . . . Then why the present discrepancy—the radical break with this historical distinction of the Baptist heritage?"[10]

He then lists various possibilities, including that "too many listened too long to those with a 'takeover mentality,' whose only answer appears to be rooted not in the gospel but in 'law' and the force of law."[11]

In a book of essays published jointly by Roman Catholics and evangelicals, Southern Baptist leader Richard Land (who signed *Catholics and Evangelicals Together*) attacked the phrase "separation of church and state." He said that "for the modern-day Supreme Court to elevate a figure of speech from a letter by a President who had nothing to do with either the framing or the adoption of the First Amendment to the status of *the* interpretive standard for establishment clause doctrine says more about the philosophies and views of twentieth-century Supreme Court justices than those of the First Amendment's original eighteenth-century framers."[12]

The about-face is even more remarkable considering Baptist history. Baptists, both in the Old and the New World, faced terrible persecution, which explains their once-fervent advocacy of church-state separation. Many Baptists trace their spiritual roots to the Anabaptists, Reformation Christians who rejected the established church's ties to the state in favor of voluntaryism and of individual autonomy in religion.

"The Anabaptists plagued the mainline Protestants and the Catholics for one basic reason," wrote historian Clyde Manschreck. "They endangered the union of church and state. . . . The established church and state rationalized that for the good of society Anabaptists had to be eradicated."[13] Even Martin Luther agreed that it was right to kill Anabaptists, and Zwingli drowned them by the boatloads.

Baptists were jailed, fined, even martyred for their faith in seventeenth-century England. For this reason, some of the earliest, and clearest, expressions on religious freedom came from the pens of British Baptists.[14]

In most early American colonies with an established church, Baptists were beaten, exiled, mobbed, fined, and jailed, most often for refusal to obtain a license to preach, refusal to attend established churches, or refusal to pay taxes to established religion. The latter charge seemed most hypocritical, especially as the colonies were agitated over taxes levied by the British Parliament, though they had no representation there. Yet many who were crying about "taxation without representation" were persecuting Baptists who refused to pay a "religious tax" for a church that they weren't members of and that promulgated views they disbelieved.

"All America are alarmed at the tea tax," wrote Baptist preacher Isaac Backus, "though, if they please, they can avoid it by not buying the tea; but we have no such liberty."[15]

Under the established Anglican church in Virginia, one Baptist minister was pulled from his pulpit and, as he began to pray, the sheriff jammed the handle of a horsewhip down his throat before beating him. In 1771, four Baptists were convicted of unlawful assembly for having held a religious meeting "under the pretense of the exercise of Religion in other manner than according to the Liturgy and Practice of the Church of England."[16] For the crime of "preaching the gospel" contrary to the Anglican Book of Common Prayer, a Baptist preacher spent forty-six days in jail.

Persecution of Virginia Baptists caused young James Madison to write to a friend "that diabolical Hell-conceived principle of persecution rages . . . and to their eternal Infamy the Clergy can furnish their quota of Imps for such business. This vexes me the most of any thing whatever. There are at this [time] in the adjacent County not less than 5 or 6 well meaning men in close Goal [jail] for publishing their religious Sentiments which in the main are very orthodox. . . . I have squabbled and scolded abused and ridiculed so long about it, [to so lit]tle purpose that I am without common patience. So I [leave you] to pity me and pray for Liberty of Conscience [to revive among us.]"[17]

No wonder that after the 1787 Constitutional Convention submitted the document to the states for ratification, Virginia Baptists insisted that it include a Bill of Rights protecting religious freedom, or they wouldn't support ratification.

As the document originally read, it said nothing about religion, except for Article VI, clause 3: "No religious test shall ever be required as a qualification to any office or public trust under the United States." Though the states were abolishing or modifying their religious establishments, some still restricted public offices to Protestants, or at least to theists, and this clause was written to stop that abuse at the federal level. Some complained back then that, because of this clause, "pagans, deists and Mohametans might obtain office among us, and the senators and representatives might all be pagans."[18] Even today, some critics say that this clause should have never been included in the Constitution: "Having no religious test," wrote Gary DeMar in *Biblical Worldview*, "was a mistake that our nation one day will regret."[19]

Nevertheless, for Virginia Baptists, the religious test clause wasn't sufficient. Though Virginia had in 1785 passed Jefferson's "Bill for Establishing Religious Freedom," which ensured protection against state persecution on the basis of religion, the Baptists weren't about to willingly subject themselves to another government, an experimental one at that, without specific protections.

"Religious Liberty, is not sufficiently secured," complained itinerant Baptist minister John Leland about the Constitution. "No Religious test is Required as qualification to fill any office under the United States, but if a Majority of Congress with the President favour one System more than another, they may oblige all others to pay to the support of their System as much as they please, and if Oppression does not ensue, it will be owing to the Mildness of Administration, and not to any Constitutional defense, and if the manners of people are so far Corrupted, that they cannot live by Republican principles, it is Very Dangerous leaving Religious Liberty at their Mercy."[20]

How could the Founding Fathers, who sought to establish a nation—for the first time in history—on the principle that humans had God-given freedoms that no government had the right to infringe upon, write a Constitution that originally gave no explicit protection to most basic of those freedoms: religious liberty?

The Constitution, as penned in 1787, didn't specifically give any guarantees of religious liberty and church-state separation, because these principles were already inherent in the document itself, not by what it said, but by what it *didn't*. The proposed federal government was a limited government, which meant that it didn't begin with assumed or inherent powers. It could do only those things that were specifically granted to it by the Constitution itself.

"The powers delegated by the proposed Constitution to the federal government," wrote James Madison in *The Federalist Papers*, "are few and defined."[21]

Thus, because none of those "few and defined" powers in the Constitution granted the federal government the right to legislate—in any matter whatsoever—on religion (the only time religion was even mentioned was in Article VI), the framers saw no need to restrict the federal government regarding religion. Why forbid the government to do what it was never allowed to do from the start? Why should Colorado make a law that forbids Florida from issuing Colorado driver's licenses, when Florida never had that right to begin with? For the same reason, framers like Madison saw no need to include religious freedom provisions in the Constitution.

North Carolina delegate to the Philadelphia convention Richard Spaight said that "[n]o power is given to the general government to interfere with it [religion] at all. Any act of Congress on this subject would be a usurpation."[22]

Thus, inherently, the Constitution—even without the Bill of Rights—promoted separation of church and state. How much more separate can church and state be if the state, in this case, the federal one, had been given no power to legislate on religious matters? The nature of the document itself attests to the framers' devotion to keeping government separate from religion.

"I hope Congress," wrote John Adams, "will never meddle with religion further than to say their own prayers."[23]

Thomas Jefferson wrote that "certainly, no power to prescribe any religious exercise, or to assume authority in religious discipline, has been delegated to the general government."[24] The Baptists, however, weren't ready to gamble their religious freedom on the unwritten assumption that the new government would take prerogatives only specifically granted to it, and no more. Either the Constitution had a Bill of Rights protecting religious freedom, or they wouldn't support it.

Madison acquiesced. The Baptists had clout in Virginia, and if such a large and influential state refused to ratify the new Constitution, other states could have followed, and the plan for a national government uniting the states could have failed. For Madison and other federalists, this could have spelled the demise of the new country and the hopes of all who were looking to the fledgling republic as proof of whether, as Hamilton wrote, "men are really capable or not of establishing good government from reflection and choice, or whether they are forever destined to depend upon their political constitutions by accidents and force."[25] (Plus, congressional elections were coming, and the Baptists—previously enthusiastic supporters of Madison—were threatening to back his challenger, James Monroe, for the seat if he didn't support a Bill of Rights.)

Thus, the beloved, quoted, and much-admired First Amendment —the cornerstone of religious liberty (often called "Our First Liberty")—resulted not only from a political compromise and some self-serving "politicking" by James Madison, but also from the lobbying efforts of a Christian denomination looking out for number one.

"Those who think that church involvement in electoral politics began with Jesse Jackson and Pat Robertson," wrote constitutional scholar Michael W. McConnell, "do not know their American history."[26]

Americans, then, can thank Christians, in this case, Baptists, for the inclusion of First Amendment principles of separation of church and state in the Bill of Rights. Why, then, are Christians, even many Baptists, now against it?

The Virginia Baptists wanted separation of church and state for one reason: they suffered persecution without it. As long as church and state were united, the church would use the strong arm of the state to enforce—to one degree or another—its dogmas and decrees, as well as force payment of taxes to support its institutions, something the Baptists refused to do, and thus found themselves in conflict with the law.

The established church in Virginia, of course, opposed separation. Proponents argued that because the Christian religion was crucial to inculcating the values and morals needed to maintain a civil society, the state was obligated to sustain the established church. "The hardships which such a regulation might impose upon individuals, or even bodies of men," it said, "ought not to be considered."[27]

The progeny of John Leland and Isaac Backus, meanwhile, haven't faced the persecution that their ancestors did. Despite all the New Right nonsense about persecution, New Right Christians and Southern Baptists are firmly and safely entrenched in American society. They aren't like, for example, seventh-day Sabbath keepers, whose numbers are relatively small and who don't have the electoral clout to influence legislation in their behalf, as the New Right increasingly has.

The New Right doesn't want separation of church and state any more than the established church in Virginia wanted it, because— no matter how much electoral and political power the New Right gains—the hated wall of church-state separation forms a barrier against attempts to impose religious dogma on the nation. "The very purpose of a Bill of Rights," wrote U.S. Supreme Court Justice Jackson, "was to withdraw certain subjects from the vicissitudes of political controversy, to place them beyond the reach of majorities and officials and to establish them as legal principles to be applied by the courts. One's right to life, liberty, and property, to free speech, a free press, freedom of worship and assembly, and other fundamental rights may not be submitted to vote; they depend on the outcome of no elections."[28]

According to prophecy, however, those rights, at least the ones involving freedom of worship, will not remain "beyond the reach of majorities and officials." In *The Great Controversy*, Ellen White states clearly that "even in free America, rulers and legislators, in order to secure public favor, will yield to the popular demand for a law enforcing Sunday observance. Liberty of conscience, which has cost so great a sacrifice, will no longer be respected."[29] Revelation 13, talking about the same impending persecution, says that "he had power to give life unto the image of the beast, that the image of the beast should both speak, and cause that as many as would not worship the image of the beast should be killed" (verse 14).

Revelation and Ellen White aren't musing here about shutting down the local beer joint on Sundays. "Enforcing Sunday observance" to the point that dissidents shall "be killed" is not a blue law. Worshiping the beast deals with something far beyond usual Sunday legislation.

True, some colonies did have Sunday laws that not only forbade labor, but actually enforced worship. America's first Sunday law, instituted in Virginia in 1610, said: "Every man and woman shall repair in the morning to the divine service and sermons preached upon the Sabbath day, and in the afternoon to divine service, and catechizing, upon pain for the first fault to lose their provision and allowance for the whole week following; for the second to lose the said allowance and also be whipt; and for the third to suffer death." (Interesting, America's first Sunday law mandated death, and its last one will too; though, unlike the first one, the last will be enforced.)

Massachusetts' 1650 Sunday law said that "whosoever shall frequently neglect the public *worship* of God on the Lord's-day, that is approved by this Government, shall forfeit for such default convicted of, ten shillings, especial when it appears to arise from negligence, Idleness, and Prophaneness of Spirit." In 1716, those who absented themselves from "divine worship" in the colony were fined twenty shillings.

A 1762 Georgia law mandated a fine for those who "having no reasonable or lawful excuse" missed "some meeting or assembly of religious *worship*."

Such laws haven't existed in America for centuries. Some blue laws are still enforced, but they forbid only certain activities; they don't force church attendance or "divine worship" of any kind. Thus, for prophecy to be fulfilled, America will have to take a major step backward.

Of course, according to Revelation, that is just what America does! The United States will make an "image" to the beast. The beast is the Roman Catholic Church, a power that arose long before the United States did. And because Rome for centuries enforced worship, the idea of America taking a major step backward and enforcing worship makes sense, especially because the repressive colonial laws were holdovers from an Old World mentality greatly influenced by a millennium of Roman hegemony. "Any movement in favor of religious legislation," wrote Ellen White, "is really an act of concession to the papacy, which for so many ages has steadily warred against liberty of conscience."[30] However much the Protestant Reformers hated Rome, they didn't completely break away. Sunday observance and disregard for liberty of conscience are two prominent examples.

None of this impending persecution can come, to be sure, until the principle of church-state separation is destroyed, which is why the new hostility toward separation by a growing movement should be worrisome. Some Americans have always opposed church-state separation, but they have been the radical fringe, not a movement that, according to the *Washington Post*, has become the Republican Party's "most powerful organization."[31]

Indeed, even with the perfidious wall of separation "infringing" upon the political freedoms of Christians, the New Right has made impressive political gains. If it has been able to get so far now, what could it do once the wall is down?

The New Right's heavy political involvement also disproves the argument pushed by some of its doyens, who—going back to the concept of limited government—have said that the separation of church and state meant only that the government couldn't get involved with religion. "The first amendment," wrote Tim LaHaye, "merely stipulates that government make no laws that would intrude upon the church."[32] But nothing in the Bill of Rights, they assert, forbids Christians from getting involved in politics.

Of course the First Amendment—"Congress shall make no law respecting the establishment of religion or prohibiting the free exercise thereof"—never meant to exclude anyone, including Christians, from political involvement. That's not the issue. If the Constitution forbade Christians from being involved in politics, the New Right wouldn't exist. Its mere presence disproves its own premise.

What the New Right doesn't like is that the First Amendment, particularly the Establishment Clause, keeps Christians, or any religious group, from influencing the government to the extent that the government passes religious laws. The New Right doesn't gripe much about the Free Exercise Clause, which keeps the government off its back; it's the Establishment Clause, which keeps *it* off the government's back (and the rest of the country's as well) that it hates, because that clause stops it from imposing its religious agenda on the nation.

Ultimately, for prophecy to be fulfilled, a religious agenda will somehow be imposed upon the nation. America will speak with the wrath, fire, and fervency of the Apocalypse's dragon. This change can happen only when the principles of church-state separation—which the Religious Right openly wars against—are destroyed.

---

1. Jeffery L. Sheller, "Spiritual America," *U.S. News & World Report*, 4 April 1994, 58.

2. "Pat Robertson Calls Church-State Separation 'A Lie of the Left,'" *Church & State*, January 1994, 18.

Another time Robertson was quoted in *Church and State* (February 1995), page 16, as saying: "That [meaning separation of church and state] was never in the Constitution; however much the liberals laugh at us for saying it, they know good and well it was never in the Constitution! Such language only appeared in the constitution of the communist Soviet Union."

3. David Barton, *The Myth of Separation* (Aledo, Tex.: WallBuilder Press, 1989), backcover.

4. David S. Nelson, from an undated flier distributed in 1992.

5. Quoted in undated letter by Ira Glasser, executive director of the ACLU, New York.

6. Jay Alan Sekulow, American Center for Law and Justice, *CASE Bulletin*, July 1990.

7. Quoted in *The Journal of Church and State* 35, no. 4, 935.

8. Rob Boston, *Why The Religious Right Is Wrong About Separation of Church and State* (Buffalo: Prometheus Books, 1993), 10.

9. In a foreword to William R. Estep, *Revolution Within the Revolution* (Grand Rapids, Mich.: Eerdmans, 1990), viii.

10. Ibid., 9.

11. Ibid.

12. Richard D. Land, "Witness Bearing," in *In Search of a National Morality: A Manifesto for Evangelicals and Catholics*, ed. William Bentley Ball (Grand Rapids, Mich.: Baker Book House, 1992), 84.

13. Clyde Manschreck, *A History of Christianity in the World* (Princeton: Prentice-Hall, 1974), 213.

14. Thomas Helwys, who in the early 1600s established the first Baptist Church on English soil, wrote a book called *A Short Declaration on the Mistery of Iniquity* and sent a copy of it to King James. He wrote: "We still pray for our Lord the King that wee be free from suspect. For haeving anie thought of provoking evill against them of the Romaish religion in regard of their profession, if they be true & faithful subjects of the king for wee do freely professe, that our Lord the King hath no more power over their consciences than over ours, and that is none at all; for our Lord the King is but an earthly King, and he hath no authority as a king can require no more; for mens religion to God is betwixt God and themselves; the King shall no answere for it, neither may the King be judge betweene God and man. Let them be heretikces, Turcks, Jewes, or whatsoever, it apperteynes not to the earthly power to punish them in the least measure."

However axiomatic today, these words were seditious back then. Helwys was thrown in jail in 1613 and died there three years later.

15. Quoted in Leonard Levy, *The Establishment Clause: Religion and the First Amendment* (New York, MacMillan, 1986), 2.

16. Ibid., 3.

17. Quoted in Robert Alley, *James Madison on Religious Liberty* (Buffalo: Prometheus Books, 1985), 48.

18. Quoted in Albert J. Menendez, *No Religious Test: The Forgotten Story of Our Constitution* (Silver Spring, Md.: Americans United Research Foundation, 1987), 8.

19. Gary DeMar, "Why the Religious Right Is Right . . . Almost," *The Biblical Worldview* 8, no. 1,

(November 1992): 3.

20. Boston, *Why the Religious Right Is Wrong*, 166.

21. James Madison, John Jay, and Alexander Hamilton, *The Federalist Papers*, no. 45 (New York: New American Library, 1961), 292.

22. Quoted in Levy, *The Establishment Clause*, 66.

23. U.S. Congress Staff, *American State Papers*, edited by Richard H. Kohn, 151.

24. Ibid., 174.

25. *The Federalist Papers*, no. 1.

26. Michael W. McConnell, "Taking Religious Freedom Seriously," in *Religious Liberty in the Supreme Court*, edited by Terry Eastland (Washington, D.C.: Ethics and Public Policy Center, 1993), 497.

27. Thomas E. Buckley, *Church and State in Revolutionary Virginia* (University Press of Virginia, 1977), 27.

28. *West Virginia State Board of Education v. Barnette* (1943).

29. *The Great Controvery*, 592.

30. Ellen G. White, *Testimonies for the Church*, (Boise, Idaho: Pacific Press Publishing Assn., 1948), 5:711, 712.

31. David Von Drehle and Thomas B. Edsall, "Life in the Grand Old Party," *Washington Post*, 14 August 1994, A22.

32. *Faith of Our Founding Fathers*, 10

CHAPTER FIVE

"Laws in America that mandated a day of rest from incessant commerce have been nullified as a violation of the separation of church and state. In modern America, shopping centers, malls, and stores of every description carry on their frantic pace seven days a week. As an outright insult to God and His plan, only those policies that can be shown to have a clearly secular purpose are recognized" (Pat Robertson, *The New World Order*, 236).

"Of all tyrannies a tyranny sincerely exercised for the good of its victims may be the most oppressive. It may be better to live under robber barons than under omnipotent busybodies. The robber baron's cruelty may sometimes sleep, his cupidity may at some point be satiated; but those who torment us for our own good will torment us without end for they do so with the approval of their conscience" (C. S. Lewis).

Russian novelist Feodor Dostoevsky wrote that people "cannot live without worshiping something," and one day everyone will worship either God or the beast. Which of the two we choose will be revealed by whether we keep the commandments: "Here is the patience of the saints; here are they that keep the commandments of God, and the faith of Jesus" (Revelation 14:12).

For this reason, Seventh-day Adventists have always stressed obedience to the law.

"God's people have a special work to do," wrote Ellen White, "in repairing the breach that has been made in His law; and the nearer we approach the end, the more urgent this work becomes. All who love God will show that they bear His sign by keeping His commandments."[1]

Adventists emphasize, too, that Christ's death didn't lessen the obligation to obey the law.

"The claim that Christ by His death abolished His Father's law is without foundation. Had it been possible for the law to be changed or set aside, then Christ need not have died to save man from the penalty of sin. The death of Christ, so far from abolishing the law, proves that it is immutable."[2]

And we believe that the law is a crucial element in the great controversy.

"The last great conflict between truth and error," wrote Ellen White, "is but the final struggle of the long-standing controversy concerning the law of God. Upon this battle we are now entering — a battle between the laws of men and the precepts of Jehovah, between the religion of the Bible and the religion of fable and tradition."[3]

"The controversy begun in heaven over the law of God, has been kept up upon the earth ever since Satan's expulsion from heaven."[4]

"The warfare against God's law, which was begun in heaven, will be continued until the end of time. Every man will be tested. Obedience or disobedience is the question to be decided by the whole world."[5]

Adventists, however, are far from alone in stressing the importance of God's law.

"The Christian community can no more change the Law of God than change the law of gravity. We cannot—in the name of Christ —set aside His commands. We cannot—in the name of the Christian Right—compromise what God gave Moses on Mount Sinai."[6] The author of that statement was Randall A. Terry, founder of the extremist anti-abortion group Operation Rescue.

Randall Terry is explicit: "Our goal must be simple: We must have a Christian nation built on God's law, on the Ten Commandments. No apologies."[7]

No apologies, indeed. Far from being in opposition to God's law, a key New Christian Right premise is that the Ten Commandments must form the moral basis of American society. No matter how corrupt the New Christian Right is becoming by its involvement in politics, it still believes in the Ten Commandments (or at least in a corrupted version). A corrupted law for a corrupted church. It makes perfect sense.

"A more important issue," wrote Notre Dame history professor

George Marsden, "linking the concerns of the Religious Right with the longer tradition of Christianity in American politics is the belief that God's law, as understood in conservative readings of Scripture, ought to be normative in determining the laws of the nation."[8]

An article in the *Religion News Service* about the New Right said that its political activism "is further justified, many say, by scriptural injunctions that warn of divine judgment for failing to obey God's law."[9]

New Right literature and rhetoric overflow with references to the importance of God's commandments. Advocacy for God's law, for instance, has ignited the New Right's opposition to abortion. Paul J. Hill, who shot an abortion doctor in Florida in 1994, said: "Preventing murder is clearly prescribed in the historic understanding of the sixth commandment."[10] People opposed to the law of God aren't going to picket abortion clinics while carrying signs that read "Thou shalt not kill."

In *The Myth of Separation*, New Christian Right crusader David Barton printed nine graphs charting out-of-wedlock births, violent crime, sexually transmitted diseases, divorce rates, SAT scores, and other social factors. On each graph he marked the year 1963 with the phrase "Divine Law Rejected." (The Supreme Court in *Abington v. Schempp* banned devotional Bible reading in public schools in 1963.) Barton's graphs then show the acceleration of divorce, sexually transmitted diseases, etc., that supposedly began in that year. The reason, according to Barton, is clear.

"Although many of the Justices," he wrote, "had already individually rejected Divine law standards, it was not until 1962-63 that the collective outworking of their individual philosophies was manifested in their rulings. . . . That year marked the beginning of scores of cases overturning long-standing practices stemming from Divine law."[11]

"I believe," wrote Jerry Falwell, "America has reached the pinnacle of greatness unlike any nation in human history because our Founding Fathers established America's laws and precepts on the principles recorded in the laws of God, including the Ten Commandments."[12]

"The Ten Commandments," wrote Christian activist John Whitehead, "embody the basic principles upon which the laws necessary to keep peace and order can be structured."[13]

In his book *The New World Order*, Pat Robertson wrote: "Through the history of what has been called Christian civilization, the Ten Commandments, given directly by the God of Jacob thirty-four hundred years ago to a great leader of the family of Jacob, named Moses, have been considered the heart of the universal moral law. . . . Without saying so explicitly, the Ten Commandments set the only order that will bring world peace—with devotion to and respect of God at the center, strong family bonds and respect next, and the sanctity of people, property, family, reputation, and peace of mind next."[14]

"Who would have believed," wrote Tim LaHaye, "that the Supreme Court in 1980 would uphold the decision of a Kentucky school board (in *Stone v. Graham*) that the Ten Commandments, the basis of English law and the most important code of laws ever written, were illegal to display on the walls of the public schools because they represented a religious symbol?"[15]

A Christian Coalition of Colorado brochure has a quote attributed to James Madison that reads, "We have staked the future of all of our political institutions upon the capacity of all of us to govern ourselves based upon the ten commandments of God."[16] One slight problem: no proof exists that Madison ever made that statement. Apparently, the New Right will even publish bogus quotes to sustain its position on the validity of including God's law in politics.

The late Francis A. Schaeffer, philosophical guru of the New Christian Right, wrote years ago: "Here the problem of the 1920s to the 1980s is properly spelled out. It is the attempt to have absolute freedom—to be totally autonomous from any intrinsic limits. It is the attempt to throw off anything that would restrain one's own personal autonomy. But it is especially a direct and deliberate rebellion against God and his law."[17]

Almost all New Right leaders have expressed belief in the importance of the Ten Commandments for society. They view the law, in many ways, as Adventists do: the Ten Commandments are the foundation of God's government, and the principles of these commandments should help set the moral foundation for society. Another Christian expressed it like this: "The laws of these governments should be in harmony with the law of Jehovah, the standard by which all created beings are to be judged"[18] (that Christian, by the way, happened to be Ellen White).

You don't have to be a New Right reactionary or an abortion clinic bomber to appreciate the Ten Commandments. "The Western world," wrote Vanderbilt Divinity School professor Walter Harrelson (certainly no New Righter), "must surely believe that the loss of knowledge of the Ten Commandments from our common life threatens to sweep away something vital. . . . The loss of the Ten Commandments means a loss in understanding what human liberty is, what freedom of the spirit means, and how freedom is to be maintained in the world."[19]

The loss is real too. Despite polls showing that Americans believe in the Ten Commandments, American society is deluged with murder, rape, burglary, assault, drug abuse, divorce, and sexual immorality. Whatever Americans might *believe*, they certainly aren't *living* it.

How can citizens follow the Ten Commandments when most don't even know what they are? "Americans," wrote pollster George Gallup, "say they believe in the Ten Commandments, but they can't name them."[20] If the masses are so biblically illiterate that they can't even name the Ten Commandments, they could be easily duped by religious leaders into the belief that Sunday is the day they must honor as the fourth commandment.

The New Right's profession of belief in the law of God, as well as our understanding of the future attempt to enforce "the Sunday Sabbath," make an interesting combination. While we seek to uphold God's law, could persecution come by professed Christians who accuse us of breaking that law? Will those "who keep the commandments of God" be attacked as violators of those commandments?

Though Christians differ widely in their concept of the so-called "Lord's Day," almost all who believe in Sunday do so out of reverence for the law. Sunday dogma, apologetics, and polemics almost always link the "Lord's Day" to the fourth commandment.

Southern Baptists, at their 1992 convention in Indianapolis, passed a "Resolution on Keeping the Lord's Day." It states:

> Whereas, The Creation account recorded in Genesis 2:1-13 states that God completed His work in six days and rested on the seventh day; and Whereas, The Fourth Commandment recognizes the importance of keeping one day holy; and Whereas, Jesus by example and teaching kept one day for worship; and Whereas, since much of the moral breakdown in our society has come since keeping the Lord's Day holy has been largely disregarded.

Therefore, Be it RESOLVED, That this 135th session of the Southern Baptist Convention affirms the biblical teaching concerning the Lord's Day as a matter of faith and practice."

The resolution ended with: "Be it finally RESOLVED, That Southern Baptists express concern over the continuing secularization of the Lord's Day."[21]

A leader in the Lord's Day Alliance, a group which seeks to promote Sunday worship, once wrote: "The Lord's Day is the axis upon which our nation turns. What would America do without the *Sabbath Day*? Our nation is great because of its great preachers and churches but is great also because it has not forgotten to remember the *Sabbath Day* to keep it holy"[22] (italics supplied).

A *Christianity Today* editorial urged Christians to keep the "Sabbath." The editorial quotes the Sabbath commandment in Exodus and in Deuteronomy. Sounding like an Adventist, the author writes, "But the Sabbath, even this side of the Fall, is a word of grace spoken into the lives of driven, harassed workers. It says to housewives and to account executives, to welders and to attorneys, 'You may stop now—no, you must stop now—at least for a day.' "[23]

It's not just the religious who see Sunday as the Sabbath. In an article about the liberalizing of European Sunday laws, the *Wall Street Journal* said, "Shopping legislation caught up with reality in England and Wales this past Sunday, as store owners were finally able to open their doors on the *Sabbath* without breaking the law"[24] (italics supplied).

The rationale in all these references—and others—are premised on the continuing validity of God's law. Though Adventists see ourselves as the true upholders of the law—and we are (at least as far as the Sabbath commandment is concerned)—many other Christians firmly believe in the law too. Any push among churches for Sunday laws will have its impetus in the Ten Commandments, though the arguments might be cloaked in secular terms, at least at first.

However much the issue will be the law of God versus the traditions of men and women, the contrast won't be presented so starkly. Will preachers warn the flock about the judgments of God falling upon America because of "these obstinate people who want to obey God's law" or those "troublemaking Sabbath keepers who insist on obeying the fourth commandment as it reads"?

Not likely. Instead, they'll probably use all the traditional anti-Saturday/pro-Sunday arguments about why Jesus and/or the disciples changed the Sabbath, and therefore Sunday is the day that we need to keep in order to honor God's law. Ellen White's statement that we will be accused of offending God by violation of the "Sunday *Sabbath*" implies that Sunday keeping will be linked to the law. Thus, in the name of the law, we could be persecuted.

The devil is as much serpent as dragon. "It was by deception that Satan seduced angels; thus he has in all ages carried forward his work among men, and he will continue this policy to the last. Should he openly profess to be warring against God and His law, men would beware; but he disguises himself, and mixes truth with error."[25]

Though the Bible states that King Ahab "did more to provoke the Lord God of Israel to anger than all the kings . . . before him" (1 Kings 16:33), when he was confronted by the prophet Elijah, Ahab said, "Art thou he that troubleth Israel?" (1 Kings 18:17).

"I have not troubled Israel," answered Elijah, "but thou, and thy father's house, in that ye have forsaken the commandments of the Lord and thou hast followed Baalim" (verse 18). God's faithful, like Elijah, will be accused of bringing calamities on the nation by those who, in reality, are the ones bringing the calamities because of their—not the faithful's—violation of the law of God.

"As the wrath of the people shall be excited by false charges," wrote Ellen White, "they will pursue a course toward God's ambassadors very similar to that which apostate Israel pursued toward Elijah."[26]

Jesus was attacked by the religious leaders as being a rabble rouser, of stirring up the people, and even of breaking the law. "Therefore did the Jews persecute Jesus, and sought to slay him, because he had done these things on the sabbath day" (John 5:16).

The first Christian martyr, Stephen, was accused of teaching against the law. "They stirred up the people, and the elders, and the scribes, and came upon him, and caught him, and brought him to the council, and set up false witnesses, which said, This man ceaseth not to speak blasphemous words against this holy place, and *the law*: For we have heard him say, that this Jesus of Nazareth shall destroy this place, and shall change the *customs which Moses delivered us*" (Act 6:12-14, emphasis supplied).

Numerous times, Paul faced similar accusations. In Corinth, Paul was dragged before the magistrate. "When Gallio was the deputy of Achaia, the Jews made insurrection with one accord against Paul, and brought him to the judgment seat, saying, This fellow persuadeth men to worship God *contrary to the law*" (Acts 18:12, 13, emphasis supplied). In Jerusalem as well, the same charges were lodged against God's servant. "When the seven days were almost ended, the Jews which were of Asia, when they saw him in the temple, stirred up all the people, and laid hands on him, crying out, Men of Israel, help: This is the man, that teacheth all men every where against the people, *and the law*, and this place" (Acts 21:27, 28, emphasis supplied).

Rome has almost always upheld the Ten Commandments, or at least its version of them. The Council of Trent—perhaps in response to antinomianism that had crept into the Reformation—affirmed the validity of the law of God. "If anyone says that the commandments of God are impossible to observe even for a man who is justified and in the state of grace, let him be anathema. . . . If anyone says that . . . the Ten Commandments do not pertain at all to Christians: let him be anathema."

That view prevails today as well. Catholics are among the staunchest defenders of the law of God (the revised version, anyway).

"The Ten Commandments are God's laws," says one Catholic source, "and must be obeyed as duties directly to God."[27]

"Those of us who will pass through Purgatory on the way to heaven," wrote a Catholic in 1993, "will finally agree that all God's commandments are GOOD, that they MUST BE KEPT, and that they CAN BE KEPT."[28]

The New Catholic Encyclopedia says, "Apart from the two commandments of purely positive law forbidding the veneration of images and commanding observance of the Sabbath, which were abolished and indirectly fulfilled in a higher mode of divine worship, the Commandments of the Decalogue remain as an enduring expression of the natural law and thus are contained, though surpassed as a part—modest indeed—of the New Testament law."[29]

Nothing in the Bible shows how either the second or the fourth commandment were replaced with a "higher mode" of worship. This is just Roman Catholic theology attempting to justify Sunday keeping and the "adoration" of saints.

Satan's attack on the law is subtle. Don't openly denounce it;

just change it. Either way, his purposes are fulfilled.

"That the law which was spoken by God's own voice is faulty, that some specification have been set aside, is the claim which Satan now puts forward. It is the last great deception that he will bring upon the world. He need not to assail the whole law; if he can lead men to disregard one precept, his purpose is gained. For 'whosoever shall keep the whole law, and yet offend in one point, he is guilty of all.' James 2:10. By consenting to break one precept, men are brought under Satan's power. By substituting human law for God's law, Satan will seek to control the world."[30]

Adventists have known that we will be persecuted in the name of Jesus, the New Testament, and the church. But in the name of *God's law?*

Those who will advocate punishing violators of the "Sunday Sabbath" are not going to be speaking out against the Decalogue; on the contrary, their impetus to persecute will be the conviction that God's law—with the New Testament "higher mode" of worship, or whatever justification they use for Sunday—must be kept for the nation to prosper.

"While Satan seeks to destroy those who honor God's law, he will cause them to be accused as *lawbreakers*, as men who are dishonoring God and bringing judgments upon the world"[31] (emphasis supplied).

With the mixture, then, of truth and error—the truth that God's law should be kept and the error that the fourth commandment was changed to Sunday—the final conflict around those who "keep the commandments of God and have the faith of Jesus" will unfold. Indeed, persecution will come to those who claim adherence, not only to "the faith of the Jesus," but to "the commandments of God" as well.

---

1. *Testimonies for the Church*, 6:265.

2. *The Great Controversy*, 466.

3. Ibid., 582.

"Those who keep the law of God will be one with Him in the great controversy commenced in heaven between Satan and God." (*Selected Messages*, 2:160).

"From the first the great controversy had been upon the law of God. Satan had sought to prove that God was unjust, that His law was faulty, and that the good of the universe required it to be changed. In attacking the law he aimed to overthrow the authority of its Author" (Ellen G. White, *Patriarchs and Prophets*, 69).

"Satan has been persevering and untiring in his efforts to prosecute the work he began in heaven, to change the law of God. He has succeeded in making the world believe the theory he presented in heaven before his fall, that the law of God was faulty, and needed revising" (*Selected Messages*, 2:107).

"When it was announced that with all his [Satan's] sympathizers he must be expelled from the abodes of bliss, then the rebel leader boldly avowed his contempt for the Creator's law. He reiterated his claims that angels needed no control, but should be left to follow their own will, which would ever guide them right. He denounced the divine statutes as a restriction of their liberty and declared that it was his purpose to secure the abolition of law" (*The Great Controversy*, 449).

4. *Selected Messages*, 1:316.

5. *The Desire of Ages*, 763.

6. Randall A. Terry, "Selling Out the Law of Heaven," *Washington Post*, 19 September 1994.

7. Randall A. Terry, speech during anti-abortion rally in Willoughby Hills, Ohio, July 1993.

8. George Marsden, "An Overview," in *No Longer Exiles: The Religious New Right in American Politics*, edited by Michael Cromartie (Washington, D.C.: Ethics and Public Policy Center, 1993), 12.

9. Samuel K. Atchison, "Christian Right: Not Really Christian, Not Really Right," *Religion News Service*, 8 February 1995, 13.

10. Quoted in John W. Kennedy, "Killing Distorts Pro-life Message," *Christianity Today*, 12 September 1994, 56.

11. David Barton, *The Myth of Separation* (Aledo, Tex.: Wallbuilder Press, 1989), 208.

12. Jerry Falwell, *Listen, America!* (New York: Bantam Books, 1980), 25.

13. John Whitehead, *The Second American Revolution* (Elgin, Ill.: David C. Cook Publishing, 1982), 82.

14. Pat Robertson, *The New World Order* (Dallas: Word Publishing, 1991), 233.

15. *Faith of Our Founding Fathers*, 3.

16. Christian Coalition of Colorado, undated brochure.

17. Francis Schaeffer, *The Great Evangelical Disaster* (Westchester, Ill.: Crossway Books, 1984), 21.

18. Ellen G. White, Letter 187, 1903, 5.

19. Walter Harrelson, in *Ten Commandments and Human Rights*, edited by Walter Brueggemann and John R. Donahue (Philadelphia: Fortress Press, 1989), 3.

20. Quoted in Karen R. Long, "Biblical Ignorance: Some Folks Don't Know What They Believe," *Religious News Service*, 1 July 1994, 1.

21. Resolution on Keeping the Lord's Day, Southern Baptist Convention, 9-11 June 1992.

22. James P. Wesberry, "Remember the Lord's Day to Keep It Holy," *Sunday*, July-September 1989, 4.

23. Ben Patterson, "Rest? Never on Sunday," *Christianity Today*, 19 September 1986, 16, 17.

24. James Pressley, "Sunday Shopping in England and Wales Is Liberalized, but Rules Create a Maze," *Wall Street Journal*, 8 August 1994.

25. *Patriarchs and Prophets*, 338.

26. *The Great Controversy*, 590.

27. Stanley I. Stuber, *Primer on Roman Catholicism for Protestants* (New York: National Board of Young Men's Christian Association, 1953), 50.

28. Anthony Zimmerman, "Purification Before the Beatific Vision," *Homiletic and Pastoral Review*, January 1993, 29.

29. "The Ten Commandments," *The New Catholic Encyclopedia*, 4:8.

30. *The Desire of Ages*, 763.

31. *The Great Controversy*, 591.

CHAPTER SIX

"Whosoever shall be guilty of rape, polygamy, or sodomy with a man or woman, shall be punished, if a man, by castration, if a woman, by cutting through the cartilage of her nose a hole of one half inch in diameter at the least" (proposed law in Colonial America).

"The legitimate powers of government extend to such acts only as are injurious to others" (Thomas Jefferson, *Notes on the State of Virginia*, 159).

Though the crucial issue of the great controversy deals with the character of God, it culminates around the "mark of the beast," which will be nothing but an attempt to enforce a religion-based morality on society (even if the religious base for that morality is false).

But how do we respond before things become that extreme? What about attempts to impose a religion-based morality on society today? Should we fight against *any* moral legislation that has religious underpinnings or parallels just because it might lead to Sunday persecution?

Of course not. But where do we draw the line? The death penalty for those who refuse to obey Sunday laws has obviously crossed it. But what about laws to promote morality in general, even if they have a religious background? Ellen White, after all, was—due to her religious beliefs—so antiliquor that not only did she encourage Adventists to vote for prohibition, she said that if Sabbath was the only time you could do so—do it.[1]

The idea that you can't legislate morality is ludicrous. Morality is always legislated. It is one of the few things that ever is legislated. Legislation doesn't change character, only behavior, but that's all it's meant to do. In a nation that believes in church-state separation, though, legislating morality gets sticky, because morality is always linked to religion.

Though religion varies from culture to culture, in every society, religion shapes morals, and morals shape laws. In the Ayatollah's Iran, women are forced to wear chadors because Islam (at least according to the clerics) deems it immoral to expose a woman's face in public. Ireland has strict laws against abortion because the Catholic religion deems abortion immoral. Early America had strict Sunday laws because many believed that profanation of "the Lord's day" was immoral.

"Morals and religion," wrote Lord Patrick Devlin, "are inextricably joined—the moral standards generally accepted in Western civilization being those belonging to Christianity. Outside Christendom other standards derive from other religions. None of these moral codes can claim any validity except by virtue of the religion on which it is based."[2]

"Liberty regards religion as its companion in all its battles and its triumphs,—as the cradle of its infancy, and the divine source of its claims," wrote Frenchman Alexis de Tocqueville. "It considers religion as the safeguard of morality, and morality as the best security of law, and the surest pledge of the duration of freedom."[3]

"It appears that virtue," wrote Aristotle, "is the object upon which the true statesman has expended the largest amount of trouble, as it is his wish to make the citizens virtuous and obedient to the laws."[4]

"It's very difficult," wrote philosopher Bertrand Russell, "to separate ethics altogether from politics."[5]

Early Americans linked morality and religion. Because "Americans widely believed," wrote Professor Jean Yarborough, "that religion was one of the most powerful means of instilling morality, they relied upon the churches to play an active role in forming the people for self-government."[6]

"The only foundation for a useful education in a republic," wrote Benjamin Rush, "is to be laid in RELIGION. Without this, there can be no virtue, and without virtue there can be no liberty, and liberty is the object and life of all republics."[7]

"Religion is the only solid basis of good morals," wrote Gouverneur Morris, one of the framers of the Constitution; "therefore education should teach the precepts of religion, and the duties of man toward God."[8]

"Of all the dispositions and habits which lead to political prosperity," wrote Alexander Hamilton, another framer of the Constitution, "religion and morality are indispensable supports. In vain would that man claim the tribute of patriotism, who should labor to subvert these great pillars of human happiness."[9]

Early American documents show, too, just how tightly Americans united religion and morality. In 1780, Massachusetts passed *A Declaration of the Rights of the Inhabitants of the Commonwealth of Massachusetts*. Article III begins: "As the happiness of a people, and the good order and preservation of civil government, essentially depend upon piety, religion, and morality; and as these cannot be generally diffused through a community but by the institution of the public worship of GOD, and of public instructions in piety, religion, and morality: Therefore, to promote their happiness, and to secure the good order and preservation of their government, the people of this commonwealth have a right to invest their legislature with power to authorize and require, and the legislature shall, from time to time, authorize and require, the several towns, parishes, precincts, and other bodies politic, or religious societies, to make suitable provision, at their own expense, for the institution of the public worship of GOD, and for the support and maintenance of public Protestant teachers of piety, religion, and morality, in all cases where such provision shall not be made voluntarily."[10]

The constitution of New Hampshire, in 1784, says that "as morality and piety, rightly grounded on evangelical principles, will give the best and greatest security to government, and will lay in the hearts of men the strongest obligations to due subjection."[11]

The Northwest Ordinance, passed in 1787 (the year the framers wrote the Constitution), reads in Article III: "Religion, morality, and knowledge being necessary to good government and the happiness of mankind, schools and the means of education shall forever be encouraged."[12]

Unlike most other nations for most of history, Americans wanted a government based on the consent of the people. "The fabric of American empire," wrote Alexander Hamilton, "ought to rest on the solid basis of THE CONSENT OF THE PEOPLE. The streams of national power ought to flow immediately from that pure, original fountain of all legitimate authority."[13] The people were, in essence, to choose their leaders and the direction of their government. Yet if the people were to be directly involved, they needed what the framers called "public virtue."

America's founders were heavily influenced by French *philosophe* Montesquieu, who argued that unlike a despotism, which used fear to keep people in line, republics wouldn't work unless the people were virtuous. "As virtue is necessary in a republic," he wrote, "and in a monarchy honor, so fear is necessary in a despotic government." If the nation were ruled by a hereditary despot who did whatever he pleased, a virtuous citizenry wouldn't be as important as it would where the people themselves played a major role in the government.

Thus, in a republic, the framers at least at first (they later became somewhat disillusioned and framed the Constitution in a way that reflects that disillusionment[14]), believed that in order for the experiment in republicanism to survive, the people needed to be virtuous.

"Public virtue . . . wrote John Adams, cannot exist without private [virtue], and is the only foundation of Republics "[15]

"If there be [no virtue among us], we are in a wretched situation," wrote James Madison. "No theoretical checks, no form of government, can render us secure."[16]

Not only did early Americans see the need for virtue; they weren't adverse to enforcing that virtue, either. Today, those who oppose "gay rights" or condom distribution in public schools are accused of imposing their morality upon the nation. Yet as tensions rose with England, the First Continental Congress passed laws that would make an ayatollah envy.

"Colonists were to give up," wrote Anne Withington, "horse-racing, cockfighting, all gambling, theater, and expensive entertainments of any kind. They also were to cut back on funeral expenses and to bury their dead with propriety stripped of extravagance. Colonists would not wear special mourning clothes other than a black crepe band around the arm or hat for men and a black ribbon or necklace for women, and would not give away gloves or scarves as funeral presents."[17]

Whenever the federal government now attempts to ban automatic rifles or machine guns (usually after some kook kills a dozen innocent people), some Americans holler about "Big Brother" infringing upon personal rights. Yet back then, Big Brother banned theater and the giving away of scarves at funerals!

Because of the unabashed way in which early Americans linked morality and religion (i.e., Christianity), and because they weren't adverse to legislating their Christian-based morality, the New Christian Right promotes the "Christian nation" idea. New Right books, tracts, and sermons are crammed with religious quotes from the founders, all in an attempt to prove the Christian roots of American government. But these quotes prove only that many founding fathers were religious, not that they established a Christian republic. The fact that Jefferson (who once wrote that "the day will come when the mystical generation [birth] of Jesus by the supreme being as his father in the womb of a virgin will be classed with the fable of the generation [birth] of Minerva in the brain of Jupiter"[18]— a quote the New Right rarely uses) and Washington and other founders were religious no more means that they have formed a Christian nation than does a dozen Catholic women living in the same house mean that they have formed a nunnery.

Nothing in the Constitution hints of a Christian nation. The document never even mentions the word *Christian* or *God* or *Christ* or *Providence* or *Christianity*. It uses the word *religion* only twice, both times (Article 6 and the First Amendment) to restrict government activity in that area, hardly something a Christian document would do. Even the Declaration of Independence refers to the "Creator" and "Nature's God," while America's first constitution, the Articles of Confederation—which our present Constitution replaced—talked about "the Great Governor of the world."

In contrast to the U.S. Constitution, state constitutions have been filled with references to "the Author of existence" (Pennsylvania, 1776), "God" (Maryland, 1776), "Almighty God" (North Carolina, 1776), "Almighty God" (Vermont, 1777), "the SUPREME BEING, the Great Creator and Preserver of the universe" (Massachusetts, 1780). Delaware made the constitutional provision that its public officials take this oath: "I do profess faith in God the Father, in Jesus Christ His only Son, and in the Holy Ghost, one God, blessed forevermore." The U.S. Constitution, meanwhile, if not atheistic, is certainly secular in tone. After the Constitution was presented to the states for ratification, opponents of ratification cited its secularism as a reason to oppose it!

"We formed our Constitution without any acknowledgment of God," said Yale President Timothy Dwight in the early 1800s. "The

Convention, by which it was formed, never asked, even once, his direction, or his blessing upon their labours. Thus we commenced our national existence under the present system, without God."[19]

The Constitutional Convention itself, where the document was framed, debunks the Christian nation idea as well. For five hot months in 1787, delegates at the Constitutional Convention in Philadelphia fought, bickered, threatened, compromised, and (some) even stormed out in protest. The biggest haggle concerned state representation in the federal government: the small states wanted the same number of representatives as the larger ones. When the situation came to an impasse and the entire convention was threatened with dissolution, Benjamin Franklin suggested prayer, not an unreasonable request, considering the monumental issues involved.

Indeed, though the states had just won independence from the world's greatest sea power, forces threatened them from every side. Spain, France, and England still had designs on the continent, and many states bickered with each other over issues that had caused other nations to go to war. Men like Madison, Hamilton, and Washington knew that unless the convention succeeded, there was a great danger that the states would splinter and the whole American enterprise collapse.

"Yet if friendship sufficed to hold a nation together during a war," wrote Catherine Drinker Brown,"—and to win a war—in peacetime it seemed that friendship was not enough."[20]

When George Washington tried to persuade New Jersey soldiers to swear allegiance to the United States, they refused, saying, "New Jersey is our country."[21]

The states had no uniform economy and were worse off financially after the war than before. The central government was unable to collect taxes or force the states to pay off the war debt. Because, wrote Constitutional scholar Burton J. Hendrick, the situation was at a crisis, Madison and Washington knew that "only by a strong central government could the American cause be saved."[22]

With, then, the future of the United States at stake, Franklin's humble suggestion that they implore "the assistance of heaven" seemed sensible enough, yet it met opposition. Alexander Hamilton said they didn't need "foreign aid." Franklin's request was taken to a vote—and failed! Thus, the convention that produced the Constitution of the United States of America engaged in less group prayer than any church committee would in planning a Vacation Bible School!

Perhaps the greatest evidence—outside the Constitution itself— against the Christian nation idea is the *Federalist Papers*. After the convention drafted the Constitution in September, James Madison, Alexander Hamilton, and John Jay began a series of articles in a New York newspaper under the pseudonym Publius, in which they explained the need, meaning, and ideas behind the Constitution, as well as defended it against anti-federalists, who were urging the states not to ratify (nine out of thirteen states for ratification). The eighty-five letters, composing more than 175,000 words, are called the *Federalist Papers*, "the first and still most authoritative commentary on the Constitution of the United States."[23]

The *Federalist Papers* are almost as secular as the Constitution itself. They never once use the name "Jesus Christ" or "Christian." The word *Christianity* appears once, in *Federalist #19*, in this context: "In the early states of Christianity, Germany was occupied by seven distinct nations." A handful of references to "Providence" (#2), "heaven" (#20), and "the Almighty" (#37) show that the authors believed in God, not that they were establishing a Christian republic.

The most telling refutation of the Christian nation idea was in *Federalist #69*, written by Hamilton. Responding to the anti-federalist claim by Patrick Henry and others that under the proposed Constitution the presidency would have prerogatives much like the detested king of England, Hamilton contrasted the two offices. "The President of the United States would be an officer elected by the people for *four* years," he wrote; "the king of Britain is a perpetual and *hereditary* prince. The one [president] would be amenable to personal punishment and disgrace; the person of the other [king] is sacred. . . . The one has no particle of spiritual jurisdiction; the other is the supreme head and governor of the national church."

The President has *"no particle of spiritual jurisdiction"*? How could a Christian nation have a chief magistrate with "no particle of spiritual jurisdiction"? It couldn't.

Yet even if the idea of a Christian nation is wrong, the New Right is correct on one thing: the framers wanted a moral nation, and they derived morality from religion (i.e., Christianity). When Jefferson wrote about separation of church and state, he never meant separation of morality from government, not when he wrote the law (cited at the beginning of this chapter) that mandated castration for male homosexuals and the drilling of a hole "one half inch in diameter at the least" in the nose of lesbians![24]

No matter how unorthodox his religious views (he once called the apostle Paul a dupe, an imposter, and "the first corrupter of the doctrines of Jesus"), Jefferson was still a product of his Judeo-Christian culture. Had Jefferson lived in classical Greece (far removed from the thunder and lightning of Sinai), where homosexuality was openly practiced, he might have been among the leaders and philosophers in Plato's *Symposium* who discussed "true love," especially expressed between men and boys. It could have been Jefferson, not Pausanias, who said, "Let us compare the two rules—one dealing with the passion for boys, and the other with the love of wisdom and all virtuous ways."[25]

It's hard to imagine leaders and philosophers like Madison, Jefferson, and Washington sitting around a fire in Mount Vernon or Monticello discussing homosexuality as "true love," because everything in their culture and religious background mitigated against it. Jefferson's anti-sodomy law shows that he didn't separate his religious views from his morality, nor his morality from his politics.

"No society," wrote Lord Patrick Devlin, "has yet solved the problem of how to teach morality without religion. So the law must base itself on Christian morals and to the limit of its ability enforce them, not simply because they are the morals of most of us, nor simply because they are the morals which are taught by the established Church—on these points the law recognizes the right to dissent—but for the compelling reason that without the help of Christian teaching the law will fail."[26]

But if morality is linked to religion, how does a nation that believes in separation of church and state enforce morality without enforcing religion? Does every law with a religious connection violate church-state separation? Are laws against murder unconstitutional because they coincide with one of the Ten Commandments?

Chief Justice Earl Warren wrote that

> the new line "Establishment" Clause does not ban federal or state regulations of conduct whose reason or effect merely happens to coincide or harmonize with the tenets of some or all religions. In

many instances, the Congress or state legislatures conclude that the general welfare of society, wholly apart from any religious considerations, demands such regulation. Thus, for temporal purposes, murder is illegal. And the fact that this agrees with the dictates of the Judeo-Christian religions while it may disagree with others does not invalidate the regulation.[27]

Most Adventists—even understanding that an attempt to enforce the Ten Commandments (or at least a bogus version of them) will lead to persecution—would agree with Justice Warren's rationale. But before agreeing too readily, one should realize that this rationale came from his majority opinion in *McGowan v. Maryland*, a 1961 U.S. Supreme Court case that upheld the constitutionality of Sunday laws because they merely happened "to coincide or harmonize" with a religion!

How do we—who believe in God's law—respond to attempts to promote morality based on that law, especially when Ellen White wrote that "in the law of the kingdom of God who rules the sinless inhabitants of heaven are to be found the principles that should lie at the foundation of the law of earthly governments"[28]? If religion is tied to morality, and morality is tied to politics, then inevitably religion will affect politics, and the last thing those who believe in God's law ought to do—or even appear to be doing—is fight every attempt to legislate those principles out of fear that each step brings us closer to the "mark of the beast."

Just because a state won't promote the Christian religion doesn't mean that it shouldn't promote Christian morality. If it's legitimate to legislate laws that "coincide or harmonize" with the Ten Commandments or, as Ellen White said, that are based on the principles of "the law of the kingdom of God," the issue of church-state separation becomes incredibly complex. Which commandments, or principles reflected by those commandments, are valid to legislate? If we legislate the sixth commandment, why not the fourth?

Rhode Island founder Roger Williams—centuries ahead of his time in advocacy of church-state separation—wrote that the commandments on the first tablet of the law deal with man's duty to God, while those on the second deal with man's relationship to man. The first four commandments, then, are beyond the jurisdiction of civil law, while the last six aren't.

William's distinction cleverly attempts to "render therefore unto

Caesar the things which are Caesar's; and unto God the things that are God's" (Matthew 22:21). But what business is it of Caesar's if someone covets his neighbor's house, ox, or wife? Should the government force children to honor their parents? Except in certain legal circumstances, what concern should it be to government if people lie?

Meanwhile, why don't laws exist against adultery, especially when that sin has caused so much more damage to society than, for instance, homosexuality, which—because of our religious background—has been subject to legal restrictions?

In contrast, wouldn't a day of uniform rest make sense if shown beneficial to society? Once we concede, as we must, that the state should make moral laws, even if those morals are linked to, or are parallel to, religion, then "secular" Sunday legislation becomes sensible. The fourth commandment would more easily come under the purview of government than would the tenth. For this reason, Sunday laws have been upheld as constitutional, while laws attempting to restrict covetousness, general lying, or forcing children to honor their parents, no doubt, wouldn't.

If the government should promote morality, even if that morality "harmonizes or coincides" with religion, and if a uniform day of rest is helpful to morality, why shouldn't "secular" Sunday laws be constitutional?

The fact that Sunday isn't the biblical Sabbath could make Sunday laws less offensive than would an attempt to legislate Saturday, which *is* the biblical Sabbath. Those promoting "secular" Sunday laws ought to stress that Sunday is not even biblical, thus helping diffuse the argument that Sunday laws violate the Establishment Clause. Of course, they won't.

Instead, they will argue that Sunday laws promote morals, not religion. And, however much we might disagree with Sunday legislation—they do have a point.

1. Ellen G. White, *The Des Moines, Iowa, Temperance Experience*, June 1881.
2. Lord Patrick Devlin, "Morals and the Criminal Law," in *Morality and the Law*, edited by Richard A. Wassertron (Belmont, Calif.: Wadsworth Publishing Company, 1971), 28.
3. Alexis de Tocqueville, *Democracy in America* (New York: Mentor Books, 1956), 48.
4. Aristotle. *Nichomachean Ethics*, Book 1, quoted in *From Aristotle to Plotinus*, edited by T. V. Smith (Chicago: University of Chicago Press, 1956), 78.
5. *The Quotable Bertrand Russell*, edited by Lee Eisler (Buffalo: Prometheus Books, 1993), 119.
6. Jean Yarborough, "The Constitution and Character," in *To Form a More Perfect Union*, edited by Herman Belz, Ronald Hoffman, and Peter J. Albert (Charlottesville: University Press of Virginia, 1992), 239.

7. Quoted in ibid., 243.

8. Quoted in John Eidsmoe, *Christianity and the Constitution* (Grand Rapids, Mich.: Baker Book House, 1987), 188.

9. Quoted in David Barton, *The Myth of Separation* (Aledo, Tex.: Wallbuilder Press, 1989), 123.

10. A DECLARATION OF THE RIGHTS OF THE INHABITANTS OF THE COMMON-WEALTH OF MASSACHUSETTS, 20 October 1870, 374.

11. Constitution of New Hampshire, 2 June 1784, 382.

12. Northwest Ordinance, 13 July 1787.

13. *The Federalist Papers*, no. 22, 152.

14. See Gordon Wood, *The Radicalism of the American Revolution* (New York: Vantage Books, 1991).

15. Quoted in Yarborough, *To Form a More Perfect Union*, 239.

16. Ibid.

17. Ann Fairfax Withington, *Toward a More Perfect Union: Virtue and the Formation of American Republics* (New York: Oxford University Press, 1991), 11.

18. Letter to John Adams, in *The Adams-Jefferson Letters*, edited by Lester J. Cappon (Chapel Hill, 1959), 2:594; John Murrin, "Fundamental Values, the Founding Fathers, and the Constitution," quoted in *To Form a More Perfect Union*, edited by Herman Belz, 27.

19. Quoted in Murrin, "Fundamental Values."

20. Catherine Drinker Brown, *Miracle at Philadelphia* (Boston: Little, Brown, and Company, 1966), 5.

21. Ibid., 7.

22. Burton J. Hendrick, *Bulwark of the Republic* (Boston: Little, Brown, and Company, 1937), 45.

23. Clinton Rossiter, *The Federalist Papers*, vii.

24. Quoted in Harry V. Jaffa, *Original Intent and the Framers of the Constitution* (Washington, D.C.: Regnery Gateway, 1994), 265.

25. Plato, *Symposium*, excerpted in *From Thales to Plato*, edited by T. V. Smith (Chicago: University of Chicago Press, 1956), 278.

26. Lord Patrick, *Morality and the Law*, quoted in Devlin, 48.

27. *McGowan v. Maryland* (1961).

28. Ellen G. White, letter 187, 1905, 5.

CHAPTER SEVEN

"We are under a Constitution, but the Constitution is what the judges say it is" (Governor Charles Evan Hughes, quoted in Harry Jaffa, *Original Intent and the Framers of the Constitution*, 159).

"If the policy of the Government upon vital questions, affecting the whole people, is to be irrevocably fixed by decisions of the Supreme Court, the instant they are made, in ordinary litigation between parties in personal actions, the people will have ceased to be their own rulers, having to that extent practically resigned their government into the hands of that eminent tribunal" (Abraham Lincoln, quoted in Robert A. Burt, *The Constitution in Conflict*, 1, 2).

Eighteen eighty-eight was a pivotal year for Seventh-day Adventism.

First, the church published one of the most important books since John penned the Apocalypse on Patmos eighteen centuries earlier: Ellen White's *The Great Controversy*. Second, the Minneapolis General Conference convened, where two upstart preachers kicked the legalistic hierarchy in the shins with an uncompromising message of righteousness by faith, and we've been hobbling along on that topic ever since. Finally, 1888 brought the slightly discomfiting issue of Senate Bill 2983, introduced by New Hampshire Senator H. W. Blair, "TO SECURE TO THE PEOPLE THE ENJOYMENT OF THE FIRST DAY OF THE WEEK, COMMONLY KNOWN AS THE LORD'S DAY, AS A DAY OF REST, AND TO PROMOTE ITS OBSERVANCE AS A DAY OF RELIGIOUS WORSHIP." In 1888, Adventists faced a national Sunday law.

It's hard to see, though, how this could have been anything more than *a* national Sunday law, not The Big One (i.e., death decree, mark of the beast, second coming).

First, the bill stopped the federal government only from introducing practices that would, said Blair, "destroy the Sabbath in the States. That is the object of this legislation. That is all that is undertaken here. It is simply an act proposing to make efficient the Sunday-rest laws of the State, and nothing else."[1] Bill 2983 didn't enforce general Sunday keeping but simply protected the individual state's right to enforce blue laws, as well as to grant exemptions whenever it chose.

Second, with anti-Catholicism virulent in America—how could the United States in 1888 "unite with the papacy in forcing the conscience and compelling men to honor the false Sabbath"[2]? If Catholics and Protestants have only in the past few decades begun acknowledging each other as "brothers and sisters in Christ," their uniting in the late nineteenth century to persecute Sabbath keepers seems unlikely, whatever the fate of Bill 2983.

Third, in 1888 (and the following few decades) America was not politically or militarily positioned to cause "the earth and them which dwell therein to worship the first beast, whose deadly wound was healed" (Revelation 13:12).

Yet even if the laws didn't lead to the mark of the beast, the last thing the Adventist Church wanted was legislation that strengthened or protected Sunday laws. Adventists had been arrested for painting churches, digging potatoes, cutting briars out of fences, plowing, hauling rails, cutting firewood, loading firewood on a wagon, working in a garden, hunting squirrels, and even "for hauling some window sashes for the new Seventh-day Adventist church from the steamer dock on Sunday."[3]

Because of this persecution, Adventist religious liberty advocate A. T. Jones testified on December 13, 1888, before the United States Senate Committee on Education and Labor, against Bill 2983 in the Fiftieth Congress.

In one sense, Jones had it easy. Bill 2983 was permeated with religion. Its stated purpose was to promote "the Lord's day" as "a day of religious worship." It forbade "secular labor" and sought to enhance "the religious observance of the Sabbath day." This aspect of the proposed legislation left it wide open to Jones's assault.

"The object of this Sunday bill," Jones argued before the committee, "is wholly religious. The last section shows the object of the entire bill; and that is, 'to secure to the whole people rest, . . . and the religious observance of the Sabbath day.' No one, therefore, need attempt to evade the force of objections against this bill by saying that it is not the religious, but the *civil*, observance of the day that is required; because it is plainly declared in the bill . . . that it is also to secure the *religious* observance of the Sabbath day. There is not a single reference in the bill to any such thing as the civil observance of the day. The word *civil* is not used in the bill. It is a religious bill wholly. The title of the bill declares that its object is to secure to the people the enjoyment of the Lord's day as a day of rest, 'and to promote its observance as a day of *religious worship.*' "[4]

The bill expired with the Fiftieth Congress. It probably would have died even without Jones's eloquent testimony. Though Sunday laws were still on the books in all states, they were slowly eroding, at least in practice.

America at that time was engulfed in rampant capitalism, entrepreneurship, and free enterprise. Ironically, with blue laws giving people more leisure time, Sunday—particularly for the entertainment business—was the most profitable day. As the nation grew and expanded, Americans were looking to find and create wealth. People were making money and, because Sunday laws restricted that process, sentiment increased against them.

"After the Civil War," wrote historian Alan Raucher, "businesses in many parts of the country more openly and frequently ignored or violated Sunday-closing laws. Sunday newspapers, which had appeared briefly during the war in New York and Boston, became commonplace in rapidly expanding urban areas. Restaurants, hotels, and resorts often operated on Sundays. Streetcars, railroads, and other means of transportation enjoyed a Sunday boom, with passenger traffic in some areas as heavy as during the rest of the week. In addition, several kinds of commercial entertainments on Sundays, especially baseball, won increasing public acceptance. Their successes revealed that many Americans contributed to the commercialization of Sundays and other holidays by treating them as new opportunities for buying, selling, and leisure activities."[5]

Politics, then, as much as theology, helped sink Blair's bill. Yet why was the bill written with such religious overtones? Though Establishment Clause jurisprudence wasn't to be developed until the next century, the blatant religious language certainly made the bill an easy target. Sunday-law advocates had already found, even before the Blair bill, a way to circumvent the church-state question.

"Sunday law proponents learned from these skirmishes," wrote Warren Johns. "They learned that the stronger the religious rationale advanced for creating the establishment, the stronger were the constitutional arguments available to opponents. Consequently the reformers made an effort to cultivate the support of labor on the basis that a Federal blue law would serve a public-welfare purpose and promote the interests of the laboring man."[6]

Even before Blair's bill, advocates were promoting Sunday laws as establishing secular days of rest for the well-being of society. As far back as 1797, Massachusetts passed a Sunday law because "the Lord's day is highly promotive of the welfare of a community, by affording necessary seasons for relaxation from labor and the cares of business."[7] By the mid-to-late 1800s, the secular rationale for Sunday laws was becoming part of American jurisprudence.

However oxymoronic, the term *the secular Sunday* was hatched. And though blue laws themselves, with a few exceptions, have all but gone the way of segregated toilets, the U.S. Supreme Court in 1961 handed down (in one day) four decisions that firmly established the constitutional rationale for Sunday legislation.[8] Whenever Sunday laws first return, if written correctly, they will have the protection of the courts!

"In the *Sunday Law Cases*," wrote U.S. Supreme Court Associate Justice William Brennan, "we found in state laws compelling a uniform day of rest from worldly labor [his use of the word *worldly*, as opposed, probably, to *religious*, betrays the fundamental fallacy of the argument that these are secular laws] no violation of the Establishment Clause. The basic ground of our decision was that, granted Sunday Laws were first enacted for religious ends, they were continued in force for reasons wholly secular, namely, to provide a universal day of rest and ensure the health and tranquility of the community. In other words, government may originally have decreed a Sunday day of rest for the impermissible purpose of supporting religion but abandoned that purpose and retained the laws for the permissible purpose of furthering overwhelming secular ends. . . . Even if Sunday Laws retain certain religious vestiges, they are enforced today for essentially secular objectives which cannot be effectively achieved in modern society except by designating Sunday as the universal day of rest."[9]

If Brennan's rationale was not bad enough, in *McGowan v. Maryland*, one of the four Sunday-law cases, Chief Justice Earl Warren, to help justify the decision, used a slice of history that will haunt Seventh-day Adventists, and that was—James Madison, "the Father of the Constitution," pushed a Sunday-law bill through the Virginia legislature! In other words, the man who worked to make into law these words—"Congress shall make no law respecting the establishment of religion or prohibiting the free exercise thereof"— worked to make into law these words as well: "If any person on Sunday shall himself be found laboring at his own or any other trade of calling, or shall employ his apprentices, servants or slaves in labour, or other business, except it be in the ordinary houshold [sic] offices of daily necessity, or other work of necessity or charity, he shall forfeit the sum of ten shillings for every such offence."[10]

The story gets worse though. Madison worked to secure passage of the Sunday-law bill; he did not pen the actual wording of the legislation. Thomas Jefferson did! About the same time that Jefferson wrote his ground-breaking "Bill for Establishing Religious Freedom," in which he said that "no man shall be compelled to frequent or support any religious worship, place, or ministry whatsoever, nor shall be enforced, restrained, molested, or burthened in his body or goods, nor shall otherwise suffer on account of his religious opinions or beliefs; but that all men shall be free to profess, and by argument to maintain, their opinion in matters of religion, and that the same shall in no wise diminish, enlarge, or affect their civil capacities," Jefferson also drafted Bill 84, "A Bill for Punishing Disturbers of Religious Worship and Sabbath Breakers."

Jefferson's bill called for the punishment of "*Sabbath*-breakers." *Sabbath* is a religious term, so the bill is nothing but religious. Jefferson didn't even attempt to couch the bill in secular language, as Sunday proponents do today.

"The title of Bill No. 84," wrote constitutional scholar Daniel L. Driesbach, "unequivocally states that this legislation was written to punish those who worked on the 'Sabbath' day. The religious intent of the bill is undeniable, made obvious by the use of the word 'Sabbath' as compared to a religiously neutral term like 'Sunday'. . . . In short, there is no indication that the sponsors of this legislation advanced the bill principally for a secular purpose."[11]

Jefferson's bill authorized the government to enforce the "Sabbath"—the exact thing that the principles of religious freedom, as expressed by church-state separation, are to forbid!

What's going on here?

After the colonies declared independence from Great Britain in 1776, legislators in Virginia wanted to rewrite the statutes of Virginia, harmonizing them with the principles of republican rule and stripping away, as much as they deemed appropriate, vestiges of the British monarchy. The result was the revision of 126 state laws, of which Jefferson revised forty-six, including three of the five laws that dealt with religion.

Nothing happened to the revisions until the mid-1780s, a few years after the war with England ended. At that time, Jefferson was the American minister in France, so James Madison—by then a powerful and respected Virginia politician—pushed most of the bills through the Virginia legislature, including Bill 82, Jefferson's "Bill for Establishing Religious Freedom," and Bill 84, "A Bill for Punishing Disturbers of Religious Worship and Sabbath Breakers." Both were enacted in 1786.

How could Thomas Jefferson, who, with Bill 82, helped establish the eternal principles of religious liberty, with Bill 84, advocate the punishment of Sabbath breakers? How could James Madison, such a staunch separationist—even opposing chaplains for the military and tax breaks for churches—push the Sabbath-breaker bill through the legislature? Their actions don't bode well for those who believe that Sunday laws of any kind—much less those as religious as Bill 84—are incompatible with the principles of religious liberty. Whenever Sunday laws are resurrected, this little bit of history no doubt will be too.

Unfortunately, neither Madison nor Jefferson wrote their sentiments about Bill 84, so we don't know their motives. The bill, however, was not written in a vacuum. Bill 84 was, actually, a revision of earlier laws, which required not only attendance at divine worship, but outlawed most travel on Sunday, "except to and from church." However egregious, Bill 84 was a great improvement over its predecessors.

At that time, too, Virginians didn't understand the principles involved in religious liberty. Jefferson couldn't even get his "Bill for Establishing Religious Freedom" passed until the mid-1780s. Even if he had wanted to abolish Sunday legislation, he might have known that it would have been impossible to have done anything other than revise it.

Madison, meanwhile, was an astute politician who would compromise even basic principles in order to achieve greater goals. Once, when faced with two threats to religious freedom, a bill to establish the Episcopal Church and a bill to levy taxes in support of churches, Madison—not wanting to vote "against God" twice in the same session—voted for what he believed were the lesser of two evils: the hated Episcopal establishment.

Does his vote mean that James Madison believed in established churches? Does his action prove that any attempt to establish a church today would be constitutional? Of course not. Then perhaps his support of Bill 84 should be viewed in the same way as his support of the Episcopal establishment: the lesser of two evils.

"In those circumstances," wrote Madison's scholar Robert Alley, "if he were prepared to support a bill quite noxious to him, in order to accomplish a greater good, with the conviction that the establishment of the Episcopalian Church would soon collapse of its own weight, might not Madison have adopted the same policy for Sunday laws anticipating a similar fate for No. 84 in the future?"[12]

Madison and Jefferson were "first generation" church-state separationists. Though principles regarding religious freedom and separation of church and state had been floating around for years, Madison and Jefferson were among the earliest to take these principles out of the realm of ideas and apply them to the real world, not an easy transition. If, after two centuries, America's top constitutional jurists, scholars, lawyers, and historians still battle over the meaning, scope, and purpose of the First Amendment, how much perfection should we expect from Madison and Jefferson? More than likely, neither understood all involved in the lofty principles they espoused.

Should their exception to the rule, then, be paraded as the rule? Both men owned slaves. Should all civil rights laws, therefore, be deemed unconstitutional? It's like Orville and Wilbur Wright: they invented the airplane, but no one would fault them for not understanding how the space shuttle works.

Perhaps the most important factor behind the support of Madison and Jefferson for Bill 84 was that Sunday keeping wasn't controversial. The nation was overwhelmingly Protestant and Catholic, and both groups kept Sunday.

"These laws aroused little controversy," wrote constitutional scholar Douglas Laycock, "and almost no one thought them inconsistent with constitutional guarantees of religious liberty."[13]

Not enough Sabbath keepers existed, particularly in Virginia, to make Sunday laws an issue. Had there been vocal Sabbath keepers, and had Sabbath/Sunday been as contentious as was the fight over tax assessments for churches, Madison and Jefferson—if they were to stay true to the principles they espoused—probably would have opposed the type of Sunday law that, under the prevailing conditions, they supported.

Of course, we can pontificate, rationalize, and speculate about Madison and Jefferson until the cows come home, but the uncomfortable historical fact remains: the two architects of religious liberty in America promoted the one thing Seventh-day Adventists fear the most—a Sunday law. And, almost two hundred years later, when the chief justice of the United States Supreme Court used that historical fact to uphold the constitutionality of Sunday laws, Adventists should take heed: history isn't necessarily going to be kind to our positions.

Bill 84, unfortunately, isn't our only historical/constitutional problem. The Constitution indirectly acknowledges, if not the *sanctity* of Sunday, at least its historical role as the weekly day of rest. Article 1, Section 7, deals with the procedure when Congress votes a bill and sends it to the President for signing: "If any Bill," the U.S. Constitution reads, "shall not be returned by the President within ten days (Sundays excepted) after it shall have been presented to him, the Same shall be a Law."

Sundays excepted? At the time the Constitution was written, Sunday was a religious day only, the "secular" rationale a hundred years away. Was the Constitution acknowledging Sunday rest? Article 1, Section 7, doesn't prove the constitutionality of Sunday laws; on the other hand, it's another fact that doesn't bode well for the future.

For the present, the situation is stable. Despite hype by offshoot groups that the national Sunday law is right here ready to be enacted immediately, talk in Washington, D.C., about Sunday legislation is about as common as is talk about prohibition. Even the New Christian Right, however favorably it might view Sunday laws, has not made them an issue, much less a priority, at least not yet. The only ones talking about a national Sunday law are Seventh-day Adventists, and the only ones making it appear as a legislative priority about to be sprung on us (while all the Jesuits at the General Conference hide the truth from the church) are offshoots.

Nevertheless, when Sunday laws do return, the justification, at least for secular laws (they have to start somewhere) is firmly in place. The Supreme Court erased the linchpin argument against them, which is that they are religious laws. In a single day in 1961, fifteen centuries of Sunday "sacredness" were dismissed.

"As we noted in our *Sunday Law* decisions," wrote Associate Justice William Brennan, "nearly every criminal law on the books can be traced to some religious principle or inspiration. But that does not make the present enforcement of the criminal law in any sense an establishment of religion, simply because it accords with widely held religious principles."[14]

With the religious element gone, valid arguments for secular Sunday laws do exist.

For example, imagine a struggling family man working at McDonald's. He wants to go to church on Sunday with his family, but the boss says he will be fired if he refuses to work, and he's too poor to take a chance on losing his only source of income. Shouldn't he have the basic right to go to church? If, however, Sunday legislation closed everything down, the worker is protected.

Pope John Paul II, in his encyclical *Centesimus Annus* (1991), wrote: "One may ask whether existing laws and the practice of industrialized societies effectively ensure in our own day the exercise of this basic right to Sunday rest."[15]

Sunday laws could also protect mom-and-pop operations against big chain stores that can afford to hire help seven days a week. Mom and Pop want Sundays off to go to church and rest, but they can't afford it because they would lose business to the big competitor down the block. Closing down the competition would give the small people a day to rest "without forfeiting business to large chain stores that can afford to stay open all the time."[16]

Though zoning laws protect neighborhoods from the wrong type of shops (who wants an X-rated bookstore or a cement factory on their block?), in many places residents have complained about the traffic, noise, and congestion coming from nearby Sunday business. Sunday legislation would provide relief at least one day a week, particularly the day that a majority of residents would like to rest.

"Six days a week is enough," said Robert Brenner, a Republican city councilman in Paramus, New Jersey. "We feel that the residents of our community deserve at least one day of peace and quiet."[17]

Law already exists to protect the family, i.e., medical leave, child custody, pension protection, and estate regulations. If freeing employees from Sunday work could help accomplish that goal as well, isn't that law justifiable?

Those who keep a day other than Sunday argue that these laws discriminate against them, and they do. But if one day is to be chosen to protect workers, small businesses, families, and neighborhoods, why not pick the day that a majority of Americans already acknowledge? After all, America is a democracy. If a relatively small number of Americans keep Friday or Saturday, or if some new religion decides to keep Tuesday, should all the benefits from a uniform day of rest be sacrificed to please them? In this case, must the majority be tyrannized by the minority? The U.S. Supreme Court has answered No. The benefits from a uniform day of rest, it ruled, firmly outweighed any burdens that this legislation might impose upon those who keep another day.

Of course, even coming from such august eminences as U.S. Supreme Court justices, arguments for Sunday laws are hardly foolproof.

First, no matter how much supporters may dress it in secular garb, a Sunday law is, by its nature, a religious law. One day of rest in seven is, in and of itself, a religious concept. Add to that the specific day, Sunday—the so-called "Lord's day"—and all the secular rhetoric about families, rest, recreation, etc., aside, a Sunday law is a religious law that violates the Establishment Clause. If the U.S. Supreme Court ruled that the erection of a "standing alone" manger scene (without something like Santa Clause or reindeer to desacralize it) on government property violates the Establishment Clause, it's amazing that the High Court could let stand a law forcing business to close on the generally recognized "Christian" day of rest!

"We have then in each of the four cases," wrote associate justice William O. Douglas in his dissent of *McGowan v. Maryland*, "Sunday laws that find their source in Exodus, that were brought here by the Puritans, and that are today maintained, construed, and justified because they respect the views of our dominant religious groups and provide a needed day of rest."

Second, to parallel Sunday-closing laws with laws against killing—as Earl Warren did in *McGowan*—is like paralleling a law that forbids the eating of ice cream on Tuesday with laws against arson. The state can do fine without laws that prohibit ice-cream consumption on Tuesday, but it won't survive without laws against arson. Society can do, and has done, quite well without laws mandating a day of rest, but no society could exist without laws against murder, which is why these laws exist in every society, religious or not.

Third, laws against killing don't necessarily have to be based on religion. Communist North Korea, which hardly reflects Western or Judeo-Christian values, punishes murder. Unlike a Sunday law, laws against violence—totally bereft of any religious connotations—are fundamental to any society.

Fourth, though the issue isn't as simple as Roger Williams made it, prohibitions against stealing and killing come from the part of the Ten Commandments that deal specifically with human's relationship to fellow humans, something within governmental prerogative. Sunday laws, in contrast, reflect a religious precept originating in human's relationship to God, which is outside of government prerogatives. Secular rhetoric doesn't change the fact that a Sunday law is not only a religious law, but it's one that—at its origins—deals with an aspect of religion outside the purview of governmental interference.

Fifth, Earl Warren's use of Bill 84 was faulty. It proved too much. His own Supreme Court would have struck down Jefferson's Sabbath-breaker bill—because of its overt religious nature—as a violation of the Establishment Clause. Yet Warren used that same bill to justify the upholding of Sunday laws. Bill 84 is no more related to secular Sunday laws than the Emancipation Proclamation is related to the Civil Rights Act of 1964, and for Warren to use Bill 84 to justify secular Sunday laws is specious at best, especially considering the radically different society and culture of Virginia in the 1780s from the United States in the 1960s. Nevertheless, Warren was chief justice, and with four more votes, he could do what he wanted.

What about the positive moral environment, particularly for the family, that would be fostered by Sunday laws? Where's the evidence that Sunday laws would strengthen the family or society as a whole? Look at our own church, in which we, voluntarily, have one day a week for rest. The "Adventist home" today—at least in North America—suffers from drug use, divorce, sexual abuse, spousal abuse, and a host of other ills found in society, almost to the same degree. Resting one day a week out of seven obviously doesn't make a family strong.

In addition, American society is radically different today than years ago, and a Sunday law might not have the anticipated moral effect. In the inner cities, for example, where unemployment is high and the family structure has been devastated—who wants gangs of bored teenagers wandering around because everything is closed on Sunday?

The bottom line is that Sunday laws, of any stripe, violate the principles not only of the Establishment Clause, but the Free Exercise Clause as well, because they make it much more difficult for those who keep another day to practice their religion.

"In other words," wrote Justice Brennan in a Sunday-law case, "the issue in this case—and we do not understand either appellees or the Court to contend otherwise—is whether a State may put an individual to a choice between his business and his religion. The Court today holds that it may. But I dissent, believing that such a law prohibits the free exercise of religion."[18]

Unfortunately, Brennan was in the minority. And, with our Sabbath practices, we are too.

However good our arguments, sooner or later, Sunday laws will be back, and with a vengeance. For now, though, the Sunday laws upheld by the Supreme Court won't give anyone the "mark of the beast." What Revelation and the Spirit of Prophecy warn about differ vastly from the typical blue law. Any attempt to enforce Sunday worship would be struck down as unconstitutional by the Supreme Court, at least as it now interprets law. Ellen White wasn't describing the Sunday legislation adjudicated in *McGowan v. Maryland* when she wrote: "It will be declared that men are offending God by the violation of the Sunday sabbath; that this sin has brought calamities which will not cease until Sunday observance shall be strictly enforced; and that those who present the claims of the fourth commandment, thus destroying reverence for Sunday, are troublers of the people, preventing their restoration to divine favor and temporal prosperity."[19]

A long distance exists between what Sunday laws have been for most of American history and what they must become in order for prophecy to be fulfilled.

But long distances, we know, can be quickly traversed.

1. A. T. Jones, quoted in *The National Sunday Law* (Boise, Idaho: Pacific Press Publishing Assn., 1888), 113, 114.

2. *Testimonies for the Church*, 6:18.

3. William Addison Blakely, ed., *American State Papers Bearing on Sunday Legislation* (1911), 656.

4. *National Sunday Law*, 45.

5. Alan Raucher, "Sunday Business and Decline of Closing Laws: A Historical Overview," *Journal of Church and State* 36, no. 1, 15, 16.

6. Warren Johns, *Dateline Sunday, U.S.A.* (Boise, Idaho: Pacific Press Publishing Assn., 1967), 72.

7. "An Act Providing for the Due Observance of the Lord's Day, and Repealing the Several Laws Heretofore Made for That Purpose," quoted in *American State Papers*, 40.

8. *McGowan v. Maryland*, U.S. 420 (1961); *Two Guys From Harrison v. McGinely*, 366 U.S. 582 (1961); *Braunfeld v. Brown*, 366 U.S. 599 (1961); *Crown Kosher Supermarket*, 366 U.S. 617 (1961).

9. *Abington School District v.Schempp*, 374 U.S. 203 (1963).

10. Report of the Committee of Revisors Appointed to the General Assembly of Virginia, 1784, Bill 84.

11. Daniel Driesbach, "Thomas Jefferson and Bills Number 82-86 of the Revision of the Laws of Virginia, 1176-1786: New Light on the Jeffersonian Model of Church-State Relation," *North Carolina Law Review* 69 (1990): 191.

12. Robert Alley, "The Madison and Jefferson Blues," *Liberty*, January-February 1995, 19.

13. Douglas Laycock, " 'Nonpreferential' Aid to Religion: A False Claim About Original Intent," *William and Mary Law Review* 27 (1986): 10.

14. *Abington School District v. Schempp*, 374 U.S. 203 (1963).

15. John Paul II, *Centesimus Annus*, printed in *Origins*, (May 1991): 21, no. 1, 6.

16. Jeanne Ponessa, "New Reasons for Blue Sundays," *Governing*, April 1994, 23.

17. William Bole, "Demise of Blue Laws Invokes Memories of Simpler Times," *Religious News Service*, 19 October 1994, 6.

18. *Braunfeld v. Brown*. Brennan Dissent.

19. *The Great Controversy*, 590.

CHAPTER
EIGHT

"The American Christian is a straight and clean and honest man, and in his private commerce with his fellows can be trusted to stand faithfully by the principles of honor and honesty imposed on him by his religion. But the moment he comes forward to exercise a public trust he can be confidently counted upon to betray that trust in nine cases out of ten. . . . His Christianity is of no use to him and has no influence upon him when he is acting in a public capacity" (Mark Twain, *Christian Science*, 359-361).

First (to reiterate where we've been), only a corrupt, but politically potent, Christianity will cause America to speak like a dragon. The New Christian Right is both: potent, as the 1994 midterm elections prove; and corrupt, as shown not only by its attempt to pawn off American Christians as martyrs but by its hostility to church-state separation (itself an interesting development in light of Bible prophecy).

Second, no matter how corrupt, the New Christian Right still has enough Christianity to believe in the validity of the Ten Commandments (even if not enough to believe in the right version).

Third, morality is always linked to religion, and in America the preeminent religion is Christianity. Morality in America, therefore, is tied to Christianity.

Fourth, if the American government has a right, even a responsibility, to make moral laws, then those laws will, to some degree, reflect Christianity.

Finally, if a secular day of rest—ruled constitutional by the U.S. Supreme Court—is helpful to society and morality, and if government has a responsibility to make laws helpful to society and morality, then (the reasoning goes) government has a right to legislate a "secular" day of rest, even if it has a Christian background. And because throughout American history Sunday has been that day of rest, the government can, constitutionally, legislate a secular Sunday.

That's the easy part. The hard part is to go from there to Revelation 13. A secular Sunday law is one thing; to execute those who keep Sabbath is, radically, another. It's a big—almost incomprehensible—leap from Sunday laws, even on a national scale, to the mark of the beast.

"Heretofore," wrote Ellen White, "those who presented the truths of the third angel's message have often been regarded as mere alarmists. Their predictions that religious intolerance would gain control in the United States, that church and state would unite to persecute those who keep the commandments of God, have been pronounced groundless and absurd. It has been confidently declared that this land could never become other than what it has been— the defender of religious freedom."[1]

What's fascinating about this reference is that "religious freedom" in her day meant something vastly different than it does today. Of the more than ninety religion clause cases that have reached the U.S. Supreme Court, all but three were decided *after* Ellen White's death.[2] The vast body of decisions that has set the course for religion clause jurisprudence—upon which most of our contemporary religious freedoms rest—were adjudicated after Ellen White lived, turning the church-state debate into one that would be unrecognizable to her.

During her life, America had "a de facto Protestant Establishment," which the courts have systematically dismantled in the past fifty years. Practices that had been accepted long after her death— i.e., Bible readings in public schools, religious symbols on public property, etc.—have now been deemed unconstitutional. Religious freedom has many more safeguards now than when Ellen White wrote about religious persecution. In some ways, it's as if she had warned about the Sioux military threat; if it were implausible then, how would it seem today?

How could religious freedom in America be so drastically transformed from her day to ours, when the sixteen words of the First Amendment's religion clauses—on which those freedoms are based—have not been altered at all? The answer is easy: what has changed are not the words, but their interpretation. And that's the scary part.

Most Americans believe that our religious freedoms are imbedded in the Bill of Rights. Parents assume the First Amendment guarantees that their children will not be indoctrinated into a religious creed by public-school teachers. Adventists believe that the Establishment Clause protects us from "religious" Sunday laws. Many Americans trust that the First Amendment shields churches and synagogues from being taxed and that it protects citizens of one faith from being taxed to support another faith. We take for granted that the Constitution stops the erection of overtly sectarian symbols on public property. And all Americans know that the First Amendment protects them from an individual state making Roman Catholicism, Mormonism, or any other faith the official religion.

Yet these assumptions are all false. The First Amendment says only that "Congress shall make no law respecting the establishment of religion or prohibiting the free exercise thereof"; it says nothing about public education, tax exemption, Sunday laws, or religious symbols on public property. In fact, with the exception of tax exemption for churches, most of those other practices, including religious Sunday laws, existed for much of American history, even after the ratification of the Bill of Rights. Long after the First Amendment became the law of the land, much of what we assume it forbids was openly practiced in this country. These practices became unconstitutional only because the Supreme Court, in the twentieth century, said that they were.

"It is surprising," wrote University of Chicago Law Professor Cass Sunstein, "that many of the principles of constitutional liberty most prized by Americans were created, not by the founders, but by the Supreme Court during this century. At the very least, the understandings that have given those principles their current life are very recent creations. Indeed, for most of the country's history the liberties chartered in our Bill of Rights were sharply circumscribed. The overriding reason for their expansion has been the interpretive practices of the modern Supreme Court."[3]

Suppose, as a precursor to the "Big One," the Sunday law (or laws) that leads to the mark of the beast, Catholics and Protestants in Virginia, now "brothers and sisters in Christ," following the New Christian Right bandwagon, amass enough political power to revamp the Virginia constitution, take over the state government, and establish a generic brand of Christianity as the official

Old Dominion religion. Suppose, too, that the first law they pass, modeled after Madison and Jefferson's two centuries earlier, is called "A Bill to Punish Sabbath Breakers."

What would stop them? The First Amendment? But the First Amendment says—and meant—specifically, that *"Congress* shall make no law respecting the establishment of religion or prohibiting the free exercise thereof." The restriction was on the Federal Congress alone. At the time the Bill of Rights was written, some states still had established churches or religious requirements for public office or religious Sunday laws. None of these practices were immediately affected by the Bill of Rights, because the First Amendment limited the federal government only; it had nothing to do with the states. Indeed, the Constitution would not have been ratified if the states had thought for a moment that it gave the federal government jurisdiction over religion in their domains.

"Certainly," wrote Thomas Jefferson in 1808, "no power to prescribe any religious exercise, or to assume authority in religious discipline, has been delegated to the general government. It must, then, rest with the States, as far as it can be in any human authority."[4]

Yet if Virginia today tried to make Christianity, or some bogus New Christian Right version thereof, the official state faith, the High Court would strike that down as an establishment of religion, even though the First Amendment limited the religion-clause prohibitions to the national Congress, and the Tenth Amendment stressed that any power not given directly to the federal government remained with the states: "The powers not delegated to the United States by the Constitution, nor prohibited to it by the States, are reserved to the States respectively, or to the people."

Where, then, did the court get the authority to strike down state establishments of religion? The Supreme Court gave it to itself.

In 1868, after the Civil War, Congress passed the Fourteenth Amendment, which was to force the states to give Blacks the same procedural legal protections as Whites (jury trial, bail, habeas corpus, etc.).[5] The amendment said nothing about the Establishment and Free Exercise clauses, and the Court for decades consistently rejected attempts to use the Fourteenth Amendment as a vehicle to apply religion-clause restrictions on the states. Not until 1940—seventy-two years after the passage of the Fourteenth Amendment!—did the U.S. Supreme Court suddenly discover that the

Fourteenth Amendment did, after all, apply the Free Exercise clause to the states,[6] and in 1947 it discovered that, through the Fourteenth Amendment, the Establishment Clause applied to the states as well.[7]

The *result* of this process, at least for religious liberty, has been incalculably good. "Selective incorporation"—in which the Supreme Court selects which Bill of Rights restrictions apply to the states—has given Americans protection against state attempts to violate religious freedom. However good the ends, the means are questionable.

"By placing a limitation," wrote Professor Bernard Siegan, "on the authority of the central government to advance a national religion, the establishment clause, as originally drafted, safeguards the powers of the states to sponsor or further religions of their own choosing."[8]

"Congress was forbidden," said an article in *National Review*, "to legislate at all concerning church establishment—either for or against. It was prevented from setting up a national established church; equally to the point, *it was prevented from interfering with the established churches in the states.*"[9]

As recently as 1983, a district court in Alabama concluded that "the establishment clause of the first amendment [sic] to the United States Constitution does not prohibit the state from establishing a religion."[10] What stopped the state in that particular case was the Supreme Court's application of First Amendment restrictions on the states through the Fourteenth Amendment; otherwise, according to the district court, Alabama could establish its own religion.

Though some historical evidence does support the idea that the Fourteenth Amendment was meant to incorporate the Bill of Rights, and the issue is still contested, it did take quite a bit of judicial imagination to find in the Fourteenth Amendment the lever to force First Amendment protections—particularly the Establishment Clause—on the states.

Former associate Justice John Paul Stevens, writing about the First Amendment, said,

> A judge who strictly construes that text must find it difficult to understand how it limits the power of any governmental body other than the Congress of the United States. Even when the First Amendment is read in the light of the Fourteenth

Amendment's command that states may not deprive anyone of liberty without due process of law, the puzzlement remains.[11]

"The First Amendment," acknowledged Pat Robertson, who has jumped on this anti-incorporation bandwagon, "says . . . Congress can't set up a national religion. End of story. There is not in the Constitution, at any point, anything that applies that to the states."[12]

Conservative scholar Thomas Sowell wrote about the "past Supreme Court mental gymnastics through which Constitutional restrictions on the federal government have been stretched to apply to state governments."[13]

Chief Justice of the United States Supreme Court William Rehnquist had criticized the Incorporation Doctrine as "the mysterious process of transmogrification by which [a guarantee of the Bill of Rights] was held to be 'incorporated' and made applicable to the States by the Fourteenth Amendment."[14]

"If the Republican majority could enact," wrote columnist Samuel Francis after the 1994 elections, "a constitutional amendment to restore the Bill of Rights to its original meaning—as a restraint on the federal government, not on state and local authorities—20th century liberalism would literally be as dead as a dodo bird. No amendment or legislative act ever authorized the Incorporation Doctrine. It 'evolved' in the imaginations of liberal Supreme Court justices in this century."[15]

The question, then, is, How firm are these protections against state infringement upon religious liberty when it took the Supreme Court more than seventy years to discover these protections, when they are not specifically written in the text, when the Court at first denied these protections even existed, and when many today reject them?

How interesting, too, that a major thrust of the 1994 new Congress has been to return power to the states. Where it will ultimately go, who knows? But the debate shows that the issue of states' rights versus the power of the federal government isn't dead or static. Though it's hard to imagine the Incorporation Doctrine being abandoned—at least right away—stranger things have happened.

Sunday persecution in America could, indeed, rekindle where it burned in the past, and that is, with the states. However it comes, one fact is plain: our rights are not as secure as we would like to believe—and the problem of the Fourteenth Amendment is only the beginning.

1. *The Great Controversy*, 605.
2. Robert T. Miller and Ronald B. Flowers, eds., *Toward Benevolent Neutrality: Church, State, and the Supreme Court* (Waco, Tex.: Markham Press Fund of Baylor University, 1992).
3. Cass R. Sunstein, *The Partial Constitution* (Cambridge: Harvard University Press, 1993), 97.
4. Letter to Rev. Mr. Millar, 1808, quoted in *American State Papers*, 174.
5. Section I of the Fourteenth Amendment reads: "All persons born or naturalized in the United States, and subject to the jurisdiction thereof, are citizens of the United States and of the state wherein they reside. No state shall make or enforce any law which shall abridge the privileges or immunities of citizens of the United States; nor shall any state deprive any person of life, liberty, or property, without due process of law; nor deny to any person within its jurisdiction the equal protection of the laws."
6. *Cantwell v. Connecticut*.
7. *Everson v. Board of Education*.
8. Bernard H. Siegan, *The Supreme Court's Constitution* (New Brunswick: Transaction Publisher, 1989), 118.
9. M. Stanton Evans, "What Wall?" *National Review*, 23 January 1995, 58.
10. 544 F. Supp. 1104 at 1128 (1983), quoted in *Wallace v. Jaffree*, 472 U.S. 38.
11. John Paul Stevens, "The Bill of Rights: A Century of Progress," quoted in *The Bill of Rights in the Modern State* edited by Geoffrey R. Stone, Richard A. Epstein, Cass Sunstein (Chicago: University of Chicago Press, 1992), 25.
12. Quoted in "The Fierce, Furious March of the Fundamentalists, *Cosmopolitan*, January 1995, 160.
13. Thomas Sowell, "Prejudices of Supreme Court Become Laws," *Conservative Chronicle*, 20 July 1994, 15.
14. *Carter v. Kentucky*, quoted in Derek Davis, *Original Intent* (Buffalo, N.Y.: Prometheus Books, 1991), 21. (450 U.S. 288 [1981]).
15. Samuel Francis, "GOP Should Strike at the Roots of Judicial Activism," *Conservative Chronicle*, 7 December 1994, 13.

CHAPTER
NINE

"If ever the free institutions of America are destroyed, that event may be attributed to the omnipotence of the majority" (Alexis de Tocqueville, *Democracy in America*, 121).

"Political corruption," wrote Ellen White, "is destroying love of justice and regard for truth; and even in free America, rulers and legislators, in order to secure public favor, will yield to *the popular demand* for a law enforcing Sunday observance. Liberty of conscience, which has cost so great a sacrifice, will no longer be respected"[1] (italics supplied).

A popular demand for Sunday observance? What happened to the Supreme Court, which is supposed to protect Americans from this type of tyranny? How this institution—which exerts more power now than in Ellen White's day—will fail, who knows? What's clear is that for prophecy to be fulfilled, one of the great pillars of the U.S. republic, protection against majoritarian despotism, will be lost.

Though Americans pride themselves on their democratic government, it's really a faulty, even dangerous, way to run a country. "Democracy is the very worst form of government," said Winston Churchill, "except all those other forms that have been tried."[2]

Though the ancient Greeks invented democracy, many opposed it even then. Plato and other like-minded Athenians "all treated democracy," wrote I. F. Stone, "with condescension or contempt."[3] Thucydides warned about "committing the conduct of state affairs to the whims of the multitude."[4] Antisthenes asked the Athenians why they didn't vote that "asses were horses since they sometimes elected generals who had as little resemblance to real commanders as an ass did to a horse."[5]

97

For these Greek philosophers, the idea that the masses could rule themselves—or even pick adequate rulers—was ludicrous. If your shoes fall apart, you get a shoemaker; if you rupture your spleen, you get a doctor; but you don't get a doctor to fix your shoes or a shoemaker to fix your spleen. Why, then, should the common people, unqualified to govern, have a powerful political role?[6]

America's founding fathers, sharing this basic distrust of democracy, framed a government to reflect that distrust.

"The founding fathers explicitly took lawmaking power out of the people's hands," said an article in *Time*, "opting for a representative democracy and not a direct democracy. What concerned them, especially James Madison, was the specter of popular 'passions' unleashed. Their ideal was cool deliberation by elected representatives, buffered from the often shifting winds of opinion—inside-the-Beltway deliberation."[7]

Madison, in *Federalist #10*, warned that pure democracies would not check "the inducements to sacrifice the weaker party or an obnoxious individual. Hence it is that such democracies have ever been spectacles of turbulence and contention; have ever been found incompatible with personal security or the rights of property."[8] Roger Sherman, one of the founders, said that "the people immediately should have as little to do as may be about the government. They want [lack] information and are constantly liable to be misled."[9]

Because of their sentiments, the founders placed barriers between majoritarian passions and government rule. Presidents are not elected by direct, popular vote, but by the filter of the electoral college, a means of restraining what Madison called "a common passion or interest."[10] This "common passion" was thwarted, for instance, when three candidates for President won the popular vote but were denied the White House because they didn't have enough electoral votes.[11]

"One need not rehearse," wrote Princeton University professor Sheldon S. Wolin, "the familiar story of the numerous devices for restraining and reducing the power and participatory activity of the citizenry: indirect elections of senators [changed by a constitutional amendment in 1913] and the president; staggered terms of office for senators and a long incumbency of six years."[12]

Historian Gordon Wood wrote that the American Revolution unleashed popular forces that were unforeseen—and unwanted—by the founders, who then attempted to restrain what they had unwittingly loosened.

"The federal Constitution of 1787 was in part," he wrote, "a response to these popular social developments, an attempt to mitigate their effects by new institutional arrangements. The Constitution, the new federal government, and the development of independent judiciaries and judicial review were certainly meant to temper popular majoritarianism."[13]

Unquestionably, the most ambitious restraint on popular whims and passions was the creation of an independent federal judiciary, particularly the Supreme Court. This institution was to thwart the democratic process, at least in terms of constitutional rights. The Supreme Court can, through a simple 5 to 4 vote, strike down any law—no matter how many overwhelming millions voted for it. City ordinances, state laws, federal statutes, anything done through the political process, even voted by a vast majority, can be nullified by only five Supreme Court justices.

"If all mankind minus one," wrote John Stuart Mill, "were of one opinion, mankind would be no more justified in silencing that one person than he, if he had the power, would be justified in silencing mankind."[14]

That's the basic idea behind the Supreme Court: if a majority of Americans persuaded the House, the Senate, and the President to outlaw Sabbath keeping, the Supreme Court should stop them (which is why Ellen White's statement about a "popular demand" for Sunday worship is so disturbing). Congressmen, senators, governors, city council members, and the President can all be voted out of office by angry, ignorant masses duped by a corrupted clergy who want Sabbath keeping outlawed; Supreme Court justices— unelected and appointed for life—can't be. Not having to face voters, the justices can interpret the Constitution free (ideally) from all political concerns. Though some have expressed concern about this "countermajoritarian dilemma," it's not a dilemma. It's *supposed* to be countermajoritarian, the only way to protect people from, what Madison warned, was an "elective despotism."[15]

The idea of government, at least in the West, goes something like this: Individuals, left to themselves, cannot be trusted to respect each others' rights. Therefore, they need rulers to force them to behave. What restrains the rulers from abusing their power? A constitution, "a polite way of telling governmental authorities that their powers are limited, and that if they exceed these powers and enact certain laws we will not obey them."[16] Who interprets the

Constitution? The judges, the guardians of our rights. But the next question is, *Quis custodiet ipsos custodes?* (Who guards the guardians themselves?)

Here's the rub. Who tells the judges how to interpret the Constitutional text? The Constitution provides no absolute principles on its own interpretation. Everyone agrees on what the Constitution says, but not on what it means. Many different schools exist—originalists, interpretationists, the process school, critical legal theorists—on how to interpret the Constitution, each offering different results. Complicated theories have been expounded, from Interpretism and Neutral Principles[17] to Oliver Wendall Holmes's statement that he deemed a law constitutional unless it made him want to "puke."[18]

These aren't just esoteric philosophical debates among four-eyed legal nerds. How the judges interpret the Constitution affects our freedoms. Only from the *interpretation* of the text, not from the text itself, have we gained the rights—particularly in regard to religious liberty—that we take for granted in the twentieth century. What would happen, however, if the judges began to *reinterpret* the Constitution in a way that would curtail, or even abolish, those rights? Far from being a paranoid fear, this is what many, especially political conservatives, including the New Christian Right, want—particularly in the area of religious freedom.[19] [20]

Right now, a systematic attempt is being waged to roll back almost all Supreme Court church-state jurisprudence over the past sixty years, particularly regarding the Establishment Clause. Again: these specific religious freedoms and protections we enjoy are not explicitly in the text. They came, instead, only from Supreme Court rulings that were often "hopelessly divided pluralities."[21] Many people want these rulings reversed, including some Supreme Court justices, who—unlike the rest of us plebes—are in positions to make those reversals a reality.

"From both the free-exercise and establishment sides," warned constitutional scholar Ronald B. Flowers, "religious freedom is under such serious attack that it is in grave danger. Presidents Reagan and Bush, goaded by the Christian Right, appointed justices to the Supreme Court who placed religious freedom at risk by relegating the Free Exercise Clause virtually to the ash heap and by eviscerating the separation of church and state with various accommodationist schemes."[22]

It's one thing to apply religion-clause protections to the states; it's another to determine what those protections are. If "selective incorporation" took some fancy footwork, that's nothing compared to the fandangos, rumbas, and chachas sometimes used by the Court in deciding religious-liberty cases. As with incorporation, the problem isn't the results—which have often (though not always) been good—but with the means of getting them. It's almost like using Daniel 1 to prove vegetarianism or Matthew 5:48 ("Be ye therefore perfect, even as your Father which is in heaven is perfect") to prove the perpetuity of God's law.

Trying to make sense of the Supreme Court religion-clause jurisprudence is like simultaneously tracking the mass and velocity of subatomic particles: according to Heisenberg's uncertainty principle—it can't be done. The reasoning behind the Supreme Court decisions—including those that give us our rights—have been at times so confused, twisted, and contradictory that you get crossed-eyed reading them. One scholar called them "ad hoc judgments which are incapable of being reconciled on any principled basis."[23]

The Court will make up rules to use or ignore at leisure; or it uses, discards, and twists history to reach a desired end. The Court will render a ruling based on shoddy jurisprudence and then in later cases quote that earlier shoddy decision to justify another shoddy one. Justices quote precedents that agree with their goals while ignoring those that don't. Sometimes a majority of justices come up with the same ruling, but disagree on why. ("*Justice BLACKMUM* announced the judgment of the Court and delivered the opinion of the Court with respect to Parts III-A, IV, and V, an opinion with respect to Parts I and II, in which *Justice O'CONNOR* and *Justice STEVENS* join, an opinion with respect to Part III-B, in which *Justice STEVENS* joins, and an opinion with respect to Part VI.")[24] Justices have the same facts presented to them, read the same Constitution, have the same precedents, and yet come to different, even opposite, conclusions.

Some important decisions, upon which our freedoms hinge, have been decided by one or two votes. In other cases, some dissenting opinions—which have no force of law—make better sense than the opinion that, perhaps only by one or two votes, suddenly rules the land. Through the principle of *stare decisis* ("let the decision stand"), the Court relies heavily on precedence, yet in more than a hundred cases, the justices have reversed themselves. At times, the reasoning in a dissent of one case becomes the majority rationale in another, and vice versa. Little we rely on today will necessarily be secure tomorrow.

In the late 1780s, the anti-Federalist "Brutus" warned that the judges "will not confine themselves to any fixed or established rules, but will determine, according to what appears to them, the reason and spirit of the constitution."[25]

Centuries later, one of those judges, Robert Jackson, wrote that certain religious-freedom cases are "a matter which we can find no law but our own prepossessions."

Prepossessions? Pleasant thought—especially when their "own prepossessions" bind the whole nation. In Supreme Court decisions, might (measured in votes) doesn't necessarily make right: it just makes constitutional law, which the rest of the nation must obey. The results, particularly regarding the Establishment Clause, can get confusing.

"Aid for parochial-school textbooks is fine," wrote William Bennett; "aid for school supplies such as maps is not. Bus transportation to and from school can be provided for parochial-school students, but bus transportation to and from field trips cannot be provided. State money can pay for standardized tests in parochial schools, but not for teacher-made tests. . . . What do you do with a map that's in a textbook?"[26]

For years, the Court has used the *Lemon* test to determine Establishment Clause violations. The test says that a law must have a secular purpose and must not advance or hinder religion or cause excessive entanglement between government and religion. If a law violates any one of the three, it's unconstitutional.

The Constitution, of course, says nothing about a *Lemon* test; rather, the test evolved in Supreme Court jurisprudence over the years. *Lemon* has, for the most part, done a good job in keeping the wall of separation between church and state intact. It has stopped the use of law to promote sectarian agendas, everything from religious displays on public property,[27] tax dollars for parochial schools,[28] and mandating that biblical creation be taught alongside evolution in public schools.[29]

Yet *Lemon* has problems. If, as in *Wallace* v. *Jaffree*, the High Court struck down an Alabama moment of silence law because its language might be "endorsing" prayer, what would happen to a law exempting a Seventh-day Adventist from Sunday legislation? The law could, ideally, fail the first two prongs of the *Lemon* test: it doesn't have a secular purpose (it aids Adventists), and it advances religion (it gives us special protections in carrying out our faith).

This isn't just a hypothetical problem. In *Thornton* v. *Caldor*, Connecticut passed a law that no one could be required to work on his or her Sabbath. When a Presbyterian was forced by his company to work on Sunday anyway, he sued. The Supreme Court struck down the law as a violation of the Establishment Clause, because it "has a primary effect that impermissibly advances a particular religious practice"[30] (*Lemon's* second prong). No wonder some argue that *Lemon* pits establishment against free exercise.

"The Establishment Clause," wrote scholar Michael W. McConnell, "is said to require what the Free Exercise Clause forbids."[31]

The justices will also ignore *Lemon* at whim. The Supreme Court upheld the use of tax money to pay for legislative chaplains, justifying the practice from history[32] (though it tends to ignore history when it comes to issues like religious symbols on public property). The Court noted that the same week in September 1787 that the Continental Congress finalized the language of the First Amendment, it also passed a law allocating funds to pay for legislative chaplains! Had it used *Lemon*, the Court would have no doubt struck down the law as a violation of all three prongs. In one of the latest prayer-in-school disputes, the Supreme Court never even mentioned *Lemon* but used other criteria instead.[33]

Many justices have spoken against *Lemon* and would like to discard it. Associate U.S. Supreme Court Justice Antonin Scalia called it "a ghoul in a late-night horror movie that repeatedly sits up in its grave and shuffles abroad, after being repeatedly killed and buried."[34] Instead, various alternatives—such as "endorsement" or "coercion" or even "political divisiveness" tests—have been suggested, though little agreement exists.

The point is simple: the interpretation of the Establishment Clause—one of the particularly genius principles of American religious freedom—is wobbly and under siege. The issue is not whether *Lemon* is the ultimate answer (though no one has come up with something better), but that the test itself could be dumped and whatever takes its place could radically change religious freedom in America. As long as the principles of Establishment Clause jurisprudence remain what they have been under the rubric of *Lemon*, it's not likely that the Sunday persecution outlined in the

Bible and Spirit of Prophecy could come. If *Lemon* goes, as it probably will, whatever replaces it could weaken church-state separation, making repressive Sunday legislation easier to pass.

Even the Free Exercise Clause, less convoluted than its establishment counterpart, has been shaky. For years, the Supreme Court
has used the *Sherbert* Test (named for a Seventh-day Adventist
with Sabbath problems) to determine the constitutionality of a law
challenged under the Free Exercise Clause. Under *Sherbert*, the
Court asks three questions: does a law place a burden on a person's
religious practice, does the state have a compelling reason for that
law, and does the government have an alternative, a "least restric-
tive," means of achieving its ends without burdening religious action?

As with *Lemon*, *Sherbert* is not in the Constitution. It, too, evolved.
And though *Sherbert* sounds fair, free exercise claims don't always
fare well under it.

What, for example, defines a "compelling state interest"? The
Court has said that only interests of the "highest magnitude" could
infringe on free-exercise rights. Yet what interest of the "highest
magnitude" caused the Court to rule that a state could build a road
through Indian sacred lands, virtually destroying that religion?[35]
Why was forcing a Jewish military captain to take off his skullcap
(which was part of his faith) an interest "of the highest order"?[36]
Why did the Court find a compelling state interest in forbidding a
Moslem prisoner from attending a worship service on Friday after-
noons?[37] And (this case was adjudicated before *Sherbert*, but used
some of the principles) why did the Court deem Sunday laws important enough to outweigh whatever burdens they might put on
Sabbath keepers?[38] For the religious mainstream, *Sherbert* works
fine, mostly because the mainstream doesn't need it; for others—
Jews, Indians, prisoners, or even Adventists— the situation isn't
so accommodating.

In one case, adjudicated before *Sherbert* yet applying the compelling state-interest principle, the Court upheld a law that forced
Jehovah's Witnesses children—against the religious objection of
their parents—to salute the flag in public schools. The Court
ruled that for the sake of "national security," these kids must
salute![39] Fortunately, a few years later, the ruling was reversed.[40]
The constitutional text hadn't been altered from the first case to
the second, only the interpretation had.

In the flag-salute case, the Court changed for the good; in the 1990 *Smith* decision, it changed for the worse. In *Smith*, voted 6 to 3 (though Justice O'Connor voted with the majority, she rejected its rationale), the Court dumped the "compelling state interest" concept, ruling instead that—if a law applied to everyone—any incidental infringement upon someone's free exercise was not constitutionally protected. The government, the High Court ruled, no longer has to prove any "interest" at all, compelling or not, only that it didn't write the law to specifically single out any particular religion. As with the flag-salute case, what the Free Exercise Clause said hadn't changed; what changed, by just one vote, was what it now meant.[41]

"The Court's decision," wrote church-state scholar James Wood, "was a sweeping repudiation of five decades of its own interpretation of the Free Exercise Clause and three decades of its time-honored 'compelling state interest' test."[42]

After years of haggling, Congress passed the Religious Freedom Restoration Act (RFRA), designed to undo the damage of *Smith* (how ironic that it took the legislative branch, supposedly the branch least sensitive to constitutional rights, to undo what the Court, the supposed protector of those rights, had done)—but now even the constitutionality of RFRA is being challenged. In 1994, a U.S. district court in Texas ruled that RFRA was itself unconstitutional.[43]

The issue isn't *Smith*, RFRA, *Lemon, Sherbert*, or the "compelling state interest" test; the issue is that however lofty the principles of religious freedom are *in theory*, *in reality* they are often based on shaky, vacillating, and subjective opinion that many would like to reverse, modify, or annul. *Smith* proved that what the Court gives, the Court can take away, not by erasing the words of the religion clauses, but by neutering them.

We don't face "religious" Sunday laws, not because the Constitution specifically says that they are unconstitutional, but because most people don't now want them. At least for now.

"A first point to note about the Court," wrote James V. Stephens in *Liberty*, "as we look down the road to what may be, is that it flip-flops. Constitutional principles are asserted and denied, emphasized and de-emphasized, watered down and watered up."[44]

To be fair, judges have to interpret the text *somehow*, and because the Constitution doesn't say *how*, they have to decide *how*. But they are only human and do make mistakes. Meanwhile, cases are often complex, lacking easy answers, and involving situations that the First Amendment—written in broad language—doesn't specifically address. Jurisprudence, therefore, must evolve. The question is how, and in what direction?

The constitutional dilemma is, really, the human dilemma. "Nothing is certain," said the Greek skeptic Arcesilaus, "not even that."[45] Though extreme, he did express the relativity of human knowledge. Objective reality exists (just as the constitutional text itself does), but human perceptions of that reality (and of the text) are subjective. We do, as Paul said, "see through a glass, darkly" (1 Corinthians 13:12). Mathematician Kurt Godel showed that within any logical system—even one as highly structured as mathematics (much less First Amendment jurisprudence)—"there are always questions that cannot be answered with certainty, contradictions that may be discovered, and errors that may lurk."[46] If Christians disagree over the meaning of the Ten Commandments, etched in stone by the finger of God Himself, what unanimity will exist on the First Amendment, scribbled on parchment by James Madison?

Meanwhile, language itself can be subjective. "A word," wrote Oliver Wendall Holmes, "is not a crystal, transparent and unchanging; it is the skin of a living thought and may vary greatly in color and content according to the circumstances and time in which it is used."[47]

Is a tax-funded interpreter for a deaf student an establishment of religion? Four justices said Yes; five said No. Are Bible readings in the public schools an establishment of religion? Eight said Yes; one said No. Is the refusal to exempt an American Indian from legislation outlawing peyote an infringement of free exercise? Three said Yes; six No. Is a high-school graduation speaker's public prayer an establishment of religion? Five said Yes; four No. The justices all had the same sixteen words—"Congress shall make no law respecting the establishment of religion, or prohibiting the free exercise thereof"—in front of them. They just read them differently—and those differences greatly affect our freedoms.

Besides the question of interpreting the Constitution, there's the issue of changing it. Arguing that the Supreme Court justices have perverted the Constitution, *National Review* editor John O'Sullivan argued for amending it: "So we must change the Constitution in order to restore it."[48]

"The Supreme Court's school prayer decisions," said House Speaker Newt Gringrich, "were bad law, bad history, and bad culture. It was just wrong. . . . And if the Court doesn't want to reverse itself, then we have an absolute obligation to pass a Constitutional amendment to instruct the Court on its error."

As of this writing, Congress has talked about a prayer amendment. Because the justices have consistently ruled that legislated prayer in public schools is unconstitutional, a prayer amendment would conflict with the First Amendment. The former would, basically, nullify aspects of the latter. This amendment would be tampering with the Bill of Rights, a scary prospect at best.

"No experiment should be viewed with greater alarm," wrote Samuel Rabinove of the American Jewish Committee, "than a proposal to amend, for the first time, the Bill of Rights, which has served us so well."[49]

Though the Bill of Rights itself (the first ten amendments) has never been altered, other amendments have. The Eighteenth Amendment forbade "the manufacture, sale, or transportation of intoxicating liquors" in the United States. The Twenty-First Amendment reads, "The eighteenth article of amendment to the Constitution of the United States is hereby repealed." Thus, one amendment nullified the other.

"It is an interesting question," wrote constitutional scholar Harry Jaffa, "whether 'We the people . . .' have the same inherent authority to repeal the Thirteenth [the ban on slavery], as to repeal the Eighteenth Amendment."[50]

It's an even more interesting question whether "We the people . . ." could repeal the First Amendment, as they did the Eighteenth. However it happens, "We the people . . . " will be behind a "popular demand for a law enforcing Sunday observance," and the results will nullify our constitutional freedoms, whether or not the constitutional text itself ever changes.

---

1. *The Great Controversy*, 592.
2. *The Oxford Book of Quotations*, 3rd ed., 1979, 150.
3. I. F. Stone, *The Trial of Socrates* (New York: Anchor Books, 1989), 14.
4. Quoted by Desmond Lee in the Introduction, *The Republic* (London: Penguin Classics, 1987), 27.
5. *The Trial of Socrates*, 15.
6. Plato, instead, believed that only the most able should rule and, for Plato, because philosophy was the key to true knowledge—philosophers should be kings. "There will be no end to the troubles of states, or indeed, my dear Glaucon, of humanity itself," he wrote in *The Republic*, "till philosophers become kings in this world, or till those we now call kings and rulers really and truly become philosophers" (Plato, *The Republic*, 263).

7. Robert Wright, "Hyper-Democracy," *Time*, 23 January 1995, 16.

8. James Madison, John Jay, and Alexander Hamilton, *The Federalist Papers*, 81.

9. Quoted in Burton J. Hendrick, *Bulwark of the Republic: A Biography of the Constitution* (Boston: Little, Brown, and Company, 1937), 81.

10. *The Federalist Papers*, no. 10, 81.

11. Andrew Jackson lost to John Quincy Adams in 1824, Samuel Tilden to Rutherford B. Hayes in 1876, and Grover Cleveland to Benjamin Harrison, though all three losers had more popular votes.

12. Sheldon S. Wolin, *The Presence of the Past: Essays on the State and the Constitution* (Baltimore: John Hopkins University Press, 1989), 12.

13. Gordon S. Wood, *The Radicalism of the American Revolution* (New York: Random House, 1991), 239.

14. John Stuart Mill, *On Liberty* (Indianapolis: Bobbs-Merrill Company, 1956), 21.

15. *The Federalist Papers*, no. 48, 311.

16. Everett Dean Martin, *Liberty* (New York: W. W. Norton & Company, 1930), 47.

17. See Mark Tushnet, "Following the Rules Laid Down: A Critique of Interpretism and Neutral Principles," *Harvard Law Review*, February 1983, 781-827.

18. See Philip Strum, *Louis Brandeis: Justice for the People* (Harvard, 1984), 361. Quoted in *The Bill of Rights in the Modern State*, edited by Geoffrey R. Stone, Richard A. Epstein, and Cass Sunstein, (University of Chicago Press, 1992), 447.

19. Author Tom Bethell, writing about a conservative summit in Washington, D.C., in 1993, talked about a speech given by Robert Bork. "The present Supreme Court has proved itself to be 'an activist and rather unrestrained Court,' Bork added, and he quoted the majority decision in *Planned Parenthood* v. *Casey*: 'at the heart of liberty is the right to define one's own concept of existence, of meaning, of the universe.' This was New Age jurisprudence, he declared. 'We are in a state of constitutional disorder' " (Tom Bethell, "Blithe Spirits," *National Review*, 29 March 1993, 34).

20. "There is, after all, a written Constitution of the United States," wrote scholar M. Stanton Evans, "which supposedly defines and limits the authority of the federal government, in the interest of preventing the abuse of power. To all intents and purposes—despite occasional skirmishing over a restricted set of issues—this arrangement is now defunct. In reality, we no longer have a Constitution, or anything that can be accurately depicted as constitutional law" (M. Stanton Evans, *The Theme Is Freedom: Religion, Politics, and the American Tradition* [Washington, D.C.: Regnery Publishing, 1994], 67).

21. *Wallace v. Jaffree*, 472 U.S. 38; dissent, Rehnquist, 564.

22. Ronald B. Flowers, *That Godless Court: Supreme Court Decisions on Church-State Relations* (Louisville, Ky.: Westminster John Knox Press, 1994), 138.

23. Jesse Choper, "The Religion Clauses of the First Amendment: Reconciling the Conflict," *University of Pittsburgh Law Review* 41 (1980): 680. Quoted in Joseph A. Ignagni, "Explaining and Predicting Supreme Court Decision Making: The Burger Court's Establishment Clause Decisions," *Journal of Church and State*, Spring 1994, 302.

24. *County of Allegheny v. American Civil Liberties Union Greater Pittsburgh Chapter*, 492 U.S. 573.

25. "Brutus," *The Anti-Federalist Papers and the Constitutional Convention Debates*, edited by Ralph Ketcham, (New York: Mentor Books, 1986), January 31, 1788, 295.

26. William J. Bennett, *The De-Valuing of America: The Fight for Our Culture and Our Children* (Colorado Springs, Colo.: Focus on the Family Publishing, 1994), 212.

27. *Allegheny v. ACLU*.

28. *Aguilar v. Felton*.

29. *Edwards v. Aguillard*.

30. *Thornton v. Caldor*.

31. In Stone, Epstein, and Sunstein. "Religious Freedom." Michael W. McConnell. 118.

"It is disingenuous to look for a purely secular purpose," wrote Associate Justice Sandra Day O'Connor, "when the manifest objective of a statute is to facilitate the free exercise of religion by lifting a government-imposed burden" (*Wallace v. Jaffree*).

32. *Marsh v. Chambers*.

33. *Lee. v. Wiseman*.

34. *Lambs Chapel v. Center Moriches Union*.

35. *Lyng v. Northwest Indian Cemetery Protective Association*.

36. *Goldman v. Weinberger*.

37. *O'lone v. Estate of Shabazz*.

38. *Braunfeld v. Brown.*

39. *Minersville School District v. Gobitis.*

40. *West Virginia State Board of Education v. Barnette.*

41. Though the vote in *Oregon v. Smith* was officially 6 to 3, O'Connor's stinging rebuttal of the majority rationale made the majority sentiment really 5 to 4, only one vote difference.

42. James E. Wood, "The Restoration of the Free Exercise Clause," *Journal of Church and State*, Autumn 1993, 720.

43. A United States District Court in *Flores v. Boerne* ruled that "the Religious Freedom Restoration Act of 1993 is unconstitutional" because Congress exceeded its authority in passing it. The issue is expected to make it to the U.S. Supreme Court.

44. James Stephens, Jr., "Can We Count on the Court?" *Liberty*, November-December 1977, 2, 3.

45. Quoted in Richard Tarnas, *The Passion of the Western Mind* (New York: Random House, 1991), 77.

46. Charles van Doren, *A History of Knowledge* (New York: Random House, 1991), 340.

47. *Towne v. Eisner.*

48. John O'Sullivan, "Purpose of Amendment," *National Review*, 20 February 1995, 6.

49. Samuel Rabinove, "Religion in Public Schools: What Is Permissible, What Is Not." The American Jewish Committee, New York, March 1995, 12.

50. Harry Jaffa, *Original Intent and the Framers of the Constitution* (Washington, D.C.: Regnery Gateway, 1994), 56.

CHAPTER TEN

"When fear begins to become pervasive, someone will come along on a white horse and say, 'I'll bring you order.'. . . Five more years of chaos in America and someone on a white horse will offer to bring order out of our chaos. If that happens, the result will be tyranny" (Christian author Chuck Colson, "Past Blessing, Future Hope," *Focus on the Family*, 14 January 1994).

"As long as cultural deterioration continues to manifest itself in horrible ways, evangelicals will be compelled to get active, even in ways that appall them. They'll feel absolutely obliged to do so" (New Right leader Paul Weyrich, *No Longer Exiles: The Religious New Right in American Politics*, 26).

"While the Constitution protects against the invasion of individual rights, it is not a suicide pact" (Former Supreme Court Justice Arthur Goldberg, quoted in Nat Hentoff, *The First Freedom*, 95).

At first, there were only rumors, cold whispers that rumbled within their breasts. Then, with the first arrests, their words were carried on cries.

They took E's father, at night. He was allowed only his suitcase and toothbrush. E wept until morning.

Then a curfew dropped around them. With every sunset, thousands huddled inside their houses, prisoners of half the earth's rotation.

Suddenly, the orders to evacuate broke the huddles. None could believe that this was happening, not here, not in their own country, not when they had done nothing wrong. As they scrambled, their hearts ground into low gear.

Many were forced to sell homes, businesses, and property, imme-

diately and at unfair prices. Cameras, binoculars, short wave radios, and firearms were snatched out of their hands, with no recompense. All that they had worked for all their lives was reduced to what could be carried in their arms.

The children were scared, not because they understood, but because they felt the fear of those whom they loved and trusted. Not until the soldiers came with their rifles and bayonets did many wrap around the legs of their elders and cry.

They were herded into buses, into trains, which murmured and whined—mothers, fathers, the elderly, the infirm, who murmured and whined too. Little S, only eight, sat with her family on a train for three days. The shades were pulled down. They were forbidden to look out the windows.

All, about 120,000, were taken to concentration camps. J, sixteen, got off the bus into a field of mud. Before him were barbed wire, watchtowers, and soldiers with guns. Ordered inside, they were warned that those who tried to leave would be shot.

Some families had to live in horse stalls that still smelled. Y saw teeth marks along the door of their new home. Others were crammed in long wooden buildings that looked like old chicken coops. Inside, families were cramped into small cubicles with no ceilings. Every sound, from the cry of a baby to the prayers of an adult, echoed. There were long lines for latrines, which were outside, in the heat, in the cold.

Their protests climaxed into nothing but bursts of angry air. They cited the law, which forbade the imprisonment of people who had committed no crimes, who were proven guilty of no acts, who had had no trials, but the judges closed their ears to the cries and their eyes to the law.

D was twelve when they took him and his family away. He was fifteen when freed. Feeling like strangers, they returned home.

The address, 2002 Pine Street, San Francisco.

When the Japanese bombed Pearl Harbor on December 7, 1941, their planes destroyed not only America's Pacific fleet, but any notion that Americans could always count upon the courts to protect their rights. The imprisonment of tens of thousands of American men, women, and children proved that during a time of national duress, our constitutional protections aren't worth the paper they're written on.

"In future wars," wrote scholars Alfred A. Kelly and Winfred Harbison, "no person belonging to a racial, religious, cultural, or political minority can be assured that community prejudice and bigotry will not express itself in a program of suppression justified as 'military necessity,' with the resulting destruction of his basic rights as a member of a free society. Bills of Rights are written in large part to protect society against precisely such a possibility, and insofar as they fail to do so they lose their meaning."[1]

What happened in World War II should dismiss any belief that America couldn't fulfill its prophetic role. If fear of Japan caused this nation to lock up thousands of innocent people into concentration camps, what would fear of God do?

"After each perceived security crisis ended," warned former U.S. Supreme Court Associate Justice William Brennan, "the United States has remorsefully realized that the abrogation of civil liberties was unnecessary. But it has proven unable to prevent itself from repeating the error when the next crisis came along."[2]

The background to the constitutional outrage against American citizens of Japanese descent was simple. The bombing of the naval base at Pearl Harbor, besides killing thousands of sailors, left the West Coast vulnerable to Japanese attack. Meanwhile, tens of thousands of Japanese lived along the coast. Whose hearts were with the Stars and Stripes, and whose were with the Rising Sun? Who could tell? Therefore, we had to round them all up.

"A Jap is a Jap," warned General John Dewitt. "It makes no difference whether he is an American citizen or not; he is still a Japanese. . . . The Japanese race is an enemy race and while many . . . have become 'Americanized,' the racial strains are undiluted. . . . Sabotage and espionage will make problems as long as he is allowed in this area."[3]

"I'm for catching every Japanese in America, Alaska and Hawaii now and putting them in concentration camps," said Congressman John Rankin on the House floor. "Let's get rid of them now!"[4]

California Governor Culbert Olson said,

There's a tremendous volume of public opinion now developing against the Japanese of all classes, that is aliens and non-aliens, to get them off the land, and in Southern California around Los Angeles—in that area too—they want and they are bringing pressure on the government to move all the Japanese out. As a matter of fact, it's not being instigated or developed by people who are not thinking but by the best people of California.[5]

Of course, a major purpose of the independent federal judiciary is to protect individual rights from this type of emotional, popular fervor. Yet when the constitutionality of the curfew against Japanese Americans, then their evacuation and imprisonment, reached the U.S. Supreme Court, the Court ruled that Roosevelt's government was within its rights. Despite the clear meaning of the Constitution itself, which says that no person shall "be deprived of life, liberty, or property without due process of law" and that no state could deny "any person within its jurisdiction the equal protection of the laws"—the arrest, evacuation, and imprisonment of 120,000 people who had been convicted of no crimes and had been given no trial (in other words, without any "due process of law" or "equal protection") but simply because of their ancestry were validated by the Supreme Court.

In *Hirabayshi* v. *United States*, which dealt only with the curfew imposed upon Japanese Americans, the Court said that

> "distinctions between citizens solely because of their ancestry are by their very nature odious to a free people whose institutions are founded upon the doctrine of equality. For that reason, legislative classification or discrimination based on race alone has often been held to be a denial of equal protection.... Distinctions based on color and ancestry are utterly inconsistent with our traditions and ideals. They are at variance with the principles for which we are now waging war. We cannot close our eyes to the fact that for centuries the Old World has been torn by racial and religious conflicts and has suffered the worst kind of anguish because of inequality of treatment for different groups. There was one law for one and a different law for another. Nothing is written more firmly into our law than the compact of the Plymouth voyagers to have just and equal laws.[6]

Nevertheless, due to the emergency situation caused by the war, the Court ruled: "We conclude that it was within the constitutional power of Congress and the executive arm of the Government to prescribe this curfew order for the period under consideration and that its promulgation by the military commander involved no unlawful delegation of legislative power."[7]

In *Korematsu* v. *United States*, which dealt with the evacuation itself, the Court acknowledged the hardship

> imposed by it upon a large group of American citizens. . . . But hardships are part of war, and war is an aggregation of hardships. All citizens alike, both in and out of uniform, feel the impact of war in greater or lesser measure. Citizenship has its responsibilities as well as its privileges, and in time of war the burden is always heavier. Compulsory exclusion of large groups of citizens from their homes, except under circumstances of direct emergency and peril, is inconsistent with our basic governmental institutions. But when under conditions of modern warfare our shores are threatened by hostile forces, the power to protect must be commensurate with the threatened danger.[8]

In a vigorous dissent, Justice Robert Jackson warned that the *Korematsu* decision was a "subtle blow to liberty." A military order in an emergency, he said, however unconstitutional, will not likely last longer than the military emergency itself.

> But once a judicial opinion rationalizes such an order to show that it conforms to the Constitution, or rather rationalizes the Constitution to show that the Constitution sanctions such an order, the Court for all time has validated the principle of racial discrimination in criminal procedure and of transplanting American citizens. *The principle then lies about like a loaded weapon ready for the hand of any authority that can bring forward a plausible claim of an urgent need*" (italics supplied).[9]

Once the principle is established that an "urgent need" allows the rights of one group to be trampled upon, what would stop another "urgent need" from trampling on the rights of another group? Though more than forty years later the United States admitted its mistake and paid reparations to the Japanese,[10] the lesson remains clear: under the right conditions, nobody's safe.

The concept of "emergency powers," which allows for the circumvention of the Constitution (such as the internment of the Nisei), was formulated and used almost from the earliest days of the United States. In the *Federalist Papers*, Hamilton wrote that

> the circumstances that endanger the safety of nations are infinite,

and for this reason no constitutional shackles can be wisely imposed on the power to which the care is committed. . . . This is one of those truths, which, to a correct and unprejudiced mind, carries its own evidence along with it; and may be obscured, but cannot be made plainer by argument or reasoning. It rests upon axioms, as simple as they are universal—the means ought to be proportioned to the end; the persons from whose agency the attainment of any end is expected, ought to possess the means by which it is to be attained.[11]

This principle has allowed the government to go outside the Constitution numerous times. The ink was hardly dry on the document when, in 1792, George Washington used emergency powers to put down a civil insurrection caused by citizens who opposed a federal whiskey tax. With the Alien Act of 1789, Congress gave the President almost unlimited power to "direct the conduct" of foreign nationals of nations hostile to the United States. Jefferson, often fearful of presidential power when he wasn't in the White House, used emergency powers as President to get around constitutional technicalities that would have hindered the Louisiana Purchase. In the wars of 1812 and 1847, special emergency powers regarding shipping, trade, and maritime commerce were enacted that allowed the government power not specifically granted to it by the Constitution.

During the Confederate revolt, Lincoln trampled on the Constitution in order, he rationalized, to save it. "I felt that measures, otherwise unconstitutional, might become lawful, by becoming indispensable to the preservation of the Constitution through preservation of the nation."[12] No President ever limited constitutional rights more sweepingly than did Lincoln during the Civil War. He suspended habeas corpus, took control of telegraph lines, restricted the travel of Confederate sympathizers, allowed unwarranted arrests by the military, confiscated the property of Confederate sympathizers, permitted the arbitrary arrest and military trials of citizens, and severely restricted free speech. In most cases, too, the Court backed up his usurpation of power.

Besides wars—strikes, economic crises, and fear of communism have each been deemed an "urgent need" that granted the President extraordinary powers.

"The United States," wrote former U.S. Senators Frank Church and Charles Mathias, Jr., in a Senate report, "thus has on the books at least 470 significant emergency powers statutes without time limitations delegating to the Executive extensive discretionary powers, ordinarily exercised by the Legislature, which affect the lives of American citizens in a host of all-encompassing ways. This vast range of powers, taken together, confer enough authority to rule this country without reference to normal constitutional processes. These laws make no provision for congressional oversight nor do they reserve to Congress a means for terminating the 'temporary' emergencies which trigger them into use."[13] The Senate report warned that "because emergency powers used in the past have tended to be authoritarian in nature, they pose a serious threat to the American democratic governmental system."[14]

Neither Scripture nor the Spirit of Prophecy, of course, detail what legalities will be used to justify end-time persecution. But the mechanisms are in place, and precedents have been set. If President Hayes in 1877 could use emergency powers to deal with a railroad strike, what would happen if the nation were reeling under the judgments of God?[15] And, according to prophecy, it's precisely that fear—of God's judgments—that will ignite persecution.

"It will be declared that men are offending God by the violation of the Sunday sabbath; that this sin has brought calamities which will not cease until Sunday observance shall be strictly enforced; and that those who present the claims of the fourth commandment, thus destroying reverence for Sunday, are troublers of the people, *preventing their restoration to divine favor and temporal prosperity.* . . . Those who honor the Bible Sabbath will be denounced as enemies of law and order, as breaking down the moral restraints of society, causing anarchy and corruption, and calling down the judgments of God upon the earth"[16] (italics supplied).

With our present government—and with the separation of church and state still intact—this scenario seems unlikely. Of course, the New Right is out to change our present government and to dismantle church-state separation. With those goals accomplished, prophecy could be quickly fulfilled.

If the U.S. Supreme Court found enough "compelling state interest" to build a road through sacred Native American land, even if that road would, the Court acknowledged, destroy that particular faith—then it could certainly view the "judgments of God" as enough of a compelling state interest to justify restrictions on the religion held responsible for those judgments.

"The impulse to make ourselves safer by making ourselves less free," wrote columnist Molly Ivins about the Oklahoma City blast, "is an old one, even here. When we are badly frightened, we think we can make ourselves safer by sacrificing some of our liberties. We did it during the McCarthy era out of fear of communism. Less liberty is regularly proposed as a solution to crime, to pornography, to illegal immigration, to abortion, to all kinds of threats."[17]

After the bombing of the federal building in Oklahoma City in April 1995, an immediate reaction arose to stifle rights in an attempt to stop domestic terrorism. However tragic, this was just one bomb, one building, and fewer people killed than die per day from smoking cigarettes. Imagine tragedies that kill ten times as many people. What would our reaction be, especially if people believed that these tragedies were caused by God's judgments?

Of course, it would be out of character, as well as be unconstitutional (as the Constitution is *now* interpreted, anyway) for our government to make theological pronouncements—such as claiming that certain disasters are the judgments of God—and then to make laws based on those pronouncements. Government in America is supposed to be neutral toward religion, and proclaiming that a flood is the wrath of God against the nation for, say, dirty movies, and then outlawing those movies in response, is not neutrality but enforcement of a specific theological doctrine.

Yet the government is composed of individuals who make, interpret, and enforce the laws—individuals who face the same fears as everyone else. If someone's house is destroyed by a flood or their family by an earthquake, "neutrality"—even for a Supreme Court justice—isn't going to be the overwhelming sentiment, especially if one believes that he or she knows the cause of the flood. If a majority of U.S. Supreme Court justices could get so caught up in the post Pearl Harbor hysteria that they gave their constitutional blessing to the internment of the Nisei, what would they do if the Potomac River were in their living rooms, caused by a judgment of God?

Even now, our country has officially recognized the existence of God. Pennies, minted by the U.S. government, display "In God We Trust." The Pledge of Allegiance includes the phrase "one nation under God." The First Congress elected a chaplain and passed a resolution asking the President to "recommend to the people of the United States a day of public Thanksgiving and prayer, to be observed by acknowledging, with grateful hearts, the many signal favors of Almighty God." Even some Supreme Court dicta have acknowledged the existence of God, one of the most famous being Justice Douglas's 1952 statement: "We are a religious people whose institutions presuppose a Supreme Being."[18] More important, at least from a prophetic standpoint, is the fact that the vast majority of Americans—94 percent—believe in God. Of all the industrialized nations, the United States is by far the most religious.

"Technology, urbanization, social mobility, universal education, high living standards—all were supposed to eat away at religion, in a wash of overlapping acids," wrote historian Gary Wills. "But each has crested over America, proving itself a solvent or a catalyst in other areas, but showing little power to corrode or diminish religion. The figures are staggering. Poll after poll confirms them: Nine Americans in ten say they have never doubted the existence of God. Eight Americans in ten say they believe they will be called before God on Judgment Day to answer for their sins. Eight Americans in ten believe God still works miracles."[19]

Of course, not everyone who believes in God or who is religious is a born-again Christian filled with the Holy Spirit. On the contrary, most aren't. Religious people have often proven just as eager and willing, if not more so than their secular compatriots, to do evil. Some of the greatest atrocities throughout history have been committed by religious people, even those adhering to the right religion. Religious people, worshiping the correct God, hung Jesus on a cross.

Pollster George Gallup has shown that most Americans who profess Christianity don't know the basics of their faith and, even more distressingly, don't act much different from non-Christians. This ignorance, he warned, is "a very frightening situation, because not being grounded in one's faith, we're open for anything that comes along"[20]— including, no doubt, the demagogues who, during economic or natural disasters, will warn that these troubles are judgments of God.

Yet, in one sense, the demagogues could be correct. From the Flood to the destruction of Sodom and Gomorrah to God's warnings against Nineveh, Egypt, Babylon, and a host of other pagan nations, the Bible clearly teaches that God's judgments do fall on rebellious nations.

> Thus saith the Lord; For three transgressions of Damascus, and for four, I will not turn away the punishment thereof. . . . Thus saith the Lord; For three transgressions of Gaza, and for four, I will not turn away the punishment thereof. . . . Thus saith

the Lord; For three transgressions of Tyrus, and for four, I will not turn away the punishment thereof (Amos 1:3, 6, 9).

The Spirit of Prophecy itself warns about the judgments of God upon the world, individual nations, and the United States.

"The point is fast being reached," Ellen White wrote, "when the iniquity of transgressors will be to the full. God gives nations a certain time of probation. He sends light and evidence, that, if received, will save them, but if refused . . . indignation and punishment will fall upon them. . . . The Lord God will soon arise in His wrath, and pour out His judgments upon those who are repeating the sins of the inhabitants of the Noachic world."[21]

"It is thus that God deals with the nations. Through a certain period of probation he exercises longsuffering toward nations, cities, and individuals. But when it is evident that they will not come unto him that they might have life, judgments are visited upon them."[22]

"We are admonished of the nearness of the end by the calamity that has befallen San Francisco. Christ declared that earthquakes and other judgments would be seen in diverse places. By these he desires to demonstrate that he hates iniquity, and that at last he will punish transgressors. He will forbear, and forbear, and forbear; but finally he can forbear no longer."[23]

If Ellen White could warn about immorality *back then!* half a century before *Ozzie and Harriet* and *Leave It to Beaver*, what would she say today, in the era of *Hustler*, MTV, and crack cocaine? Her words echo the New Right, which also has been warning about God's judgments (though it has in recent years toned down the wrath-of-God bombast). However much we will disagree with other Christians over the cause and solution to the judgments of God falling, particularly *after* the mark of the beast is enforced—for now, the New Right has a valid point when it warns about God's judgments upon iniquity and lawlessness. If Ellen White, in her day, could write that "already the judgments of God are abroad in the land, as seen in storms, in floods, in tempests, in earthquakes, in peril by land and by sea,"[24] considering the incredible decadence, immorality, and violence of contemporary America—Falwell, Robertson, and others today aren't too far off, either.

The question is not, Can the supposed "judgments of God" be used by our government to one day suppress Sabbath keepers? We know the answer already. What we don't know are the exact legal mechanisms that will be used to justify that suppression—whether emergency powers issued by the Executive Branch, a "compelling state interest" justification by the Court, or neither or both. However it comes, history—such as the internment of the Japanese—proves that even free America, in order to preserve its "best interests," will trample on constitutional protections.

Telling about her experience in one of the internment camps in the 1940s as a young woman uprooted from her home, Emi Somekawa warned about the future. "I hope that something like this will never happen to another group of people. . . . But sometimes I wonder."[25]

1. Alfred A. Kelly and Winfred Harbison, *The American Constitution: Its Origins and Development* (New York: W. W. Norton, 1955), 841.

2. Quoted in Nat Hentoff, "Tough Times for Civil Liberties," *Washington Post*, 6 May 1995.

3. Leonard J. Arrington, *The Price of Prejudice: The Japanese-American Relocation Center in Utah During World War II* (Logan, Utah: The Faculty Association of Utah State University, 1962), 6.

4. Yoshiko Uchida, *Desert Exile* (Seattle: University of Washington Press, 1982), 54.

5. Roger Daniels, *Concentration Camps USA: Japanese Americans and World War II* (New York: Holt, Rinehardt, & Winston, Inc., 1977), 51.

6. *Kiyoshi Hirabayashi v. United States*, 63 Sup. Ct. 1385, 1390 (1944).

7. Ibid., 1381.

8. *Korematsu v. United States*. In an impassioned dissent, Justice Roberts wrote that "this is not a case of keeping people off the streets at night as was Kiyoshi Hirabayashi . . . nor a case of temporary exclusion of a citizen from an area for his own safety or that of the community, nor a case of offering him an opportunity to go temporarily out of an area where his presence might cause danger to himself or to his fellows. On the contrary, it is the case of convicting a citizen as a punishment for not submitting to imprisonment in a concentration camp, based on his ancestry, and solely because of his ancestry, without evidence or inquiry concerning his loyalty and good disposition towards the United States. If this be a correct statement of the facts disclosed by this record, and facts of which we take judicial notice, I need hardly labor the conclusion that Constitutional rights have been violated" (*65 Sup. Ct.* 198 [1943]).

9. Ibid., Justice Jackson Dissent.

10. See Gary B. Swanson, "Executive Order 9066," *Liberty*, January/February 1989, 6-9.

11. *The Federalist Papers*, no. 23: Hamilton, 153.

12. Letter to Albert G. Hodges (4 April 1864) in *The Collected Works of Abraham Lincoln*, edited by Roy B. Basler, (New Brunswick: Rutgers University Press, 1953), 8:281.

13. *A Brief History of Emergency Powers in the United States: Special Committee on National Emergencies and Delegated Emergency Powers, United States Senate* (Washington D.C.: U.S. Government Printing Office, 1974), v.

14. Ibid., 120.

15. Ibid., 32.

16. *The Great Controversy*, 590, 592.

17. Molly Ivins, "Evil Cowards," *Liberal Opinion Weekly*, 8 May 1995.

18. *Zorach v. Clausen*, 508.

19. Gary Wills, *Under God: Religions and American Politics* (New York: Simon and Schuster, 1990), 16.

20. "Most Christians don't know or act their faith, Gallup says," *Religious News Service*, 10 May 1991.

21. Ellen G. White Comments, *SDA Bible Commentary* (Hagerstown, Md.: Review and Herald Publishing Association, 1978), 4:1143, 1144.

22. *Advent Review and Sabbath Herald*, 2 May 1893.

23. *Advent Review and Sabbath Herald*, 12 July 1906.

24. *Testimonies for the Church*, 5:136.

25. John Tateishi, *And Justice for All: An Oral History of the Japanese American Detention Camps* (New York: Random House, 1984), 151.

CHAPTER
ELEVEN

"In the law of the kingdom of God who rules the sinless
inhabitants of heaven are to be found the principles that should lie
at the foundation of the laws of earthly governments. The laws of
these governments should be in harmony with the law of Jehovah,
the standard by which all created beings are to be judged"
(Ellen G. White, Letter 187, 1903, 5).

"Again Jesus said, 'My kingdom is not of this world. If my
kingdom were of this world, then would my servants fight.' Every
civil law has the power of the sword back of it. If it is right to make
law, then it is right to enforce it. In denying to the church the
power of the sword, Jesus therefore forbade the church to ask the
state for laws enforcing religious beliefs and observances" (Ellen
G. White, *Watchman*, 1 May 1906).

I'm amazed, frankly, that people accept the three angels' messages—particularly the part about "the mark of the beast"—before
experiencing the Sabbath themselves, because only through the experience of Sabbath can one truly understand its significance.

Whatever the evidence from Daniel 7, where the little horn
changes God's law, and from Revelation 13, where worship of the
Creator is linked to adherence to that law (in contrast to those who
"worship the beast")—the idea that the observance of one day instead of another will outwardly symbolize who is saved and who is
lost seems, on the surface, pretty farfetched.

Once below the surface, however, where one keeps Sabbath
and experiences what it teaches about humans, God, and humans' relationship to God—the Sabbath/Sunday controversy, especially as the apocalyptic divider between the righteous and

the unrighteous, becomes powerfully obvious.

What Sabbath keeper, when Friday envelopes everything in Sabbath shadows, hasn't at some point experienced just how basic and primal Sabbath is? In a manner so powerful that—without the possibility of exception—it consumes twenty-four hours a week of our lives, the Sabbath confronts us with the realization that our life, breath, and existence come only from that Creator. Only by our experiencing the magnitude of what Sabbath contains can the day point us to what it means. By keeping Sabbath, we outwardly manifest belief that God is our Creator and Redeemer and that all we have, are, or ever could be depends upon Him. Sabbath is not just something we believe, such as the state of the dead or the sanctuary; it is something we do—and, by doing it, we not only acknowledge the sovereignty of God, we experience that sovereignty as well.

"In an arbitrary manner," wrote Raoul Dederen, "God appointed that on the seventh day we should come to rest with His creation in a particular way. He filled this day with a content that is 'uncontaminated' by anything related to the cyclical changes of nature or the movements of the heavenly bodies. That content is the idea of the absolute sovereignty of God, a sovereignty unqualified even by an indirect cognizance of the natural movements of time and rhythms of life. As the Christian takes heed of the Sabbath day and keeps it holy, he does so purely in answer to God's command, and simply because God is his Creator."[1]

By accepting without challenge God's claim to the seventh day, we honor His claim to the other six as well. If God can claim, unchallenged, one-seventh of our time, He can claim, unchallenged, all of it, because He is sovereign and, more than any other commandment, the Sabbath reveals that sovereignty.

Only after having experienced the Sabbath in all its sweeping power, only after grasping what it symbolizes about God's authority, can one comprehend—in ways that those who haven't "done" Sabbath can't—the momentous issues at stake regarding its observance.

The final controversy isn't about a day. Time, in and of itself, means nothing. God could have blessed and sanctified the first, third, or fifth day. The change of the Sabbath deals, instead, with God's sovereignty. By usurping prerogatives that belong only to God, the change usurps God Himself.

"Let no man deceive you by any means: for that day shall not come, except there come a falling away first, and that man of sin be revealed, the son of perdition; who opposeth and exalteth himself above all that is called God, or that is worshipped; so that he as God sitteth in the temple of God, shewing himself that he is God" (2 Thessalonians 2:3, 4).

If the seventh-day Sabbath is the outward sign of God's sovereignty, the first-day replacement, which sweeps away that day, sweeps away that sovereignty as well, or at least attempts to. When we experience in the Sabbath the reality of God as Creator and Redeemer and then realize that all this truth about God—which is contained in the Sabbath only because He placed it there—was usurped by a human institution, we can only shudder at the arrogance, audacity, and apostasy involved. Only then will the real issue regarding the mark of the beast be grasped.

Medieval scholar Anselm wrote, *"I believe in order that I may understand."* We need, therefore, to sympathize with those who, having never experienced the sovereignty of God through the Sabbath, don't believe and, thus, don't understand.

If, however, Sabbath is a powerful manifestation of God's sovereignty, would we then compromise our acknowledgment of that sovereignty if, compelled by strict penalties, we refrain from work on Sunday? If this nation passed a strict Sunday law mandating that Americans not violate the "Lord's Day," should we obey, even if the law was a blatantly unchristian symbol of Rome's attempt at usurping God's prerogatives?

Most Adventists don't work on Sunday anyway. If "six days shalt thou labor and do all thy work" means that we *must* work six days a week, am I violating the fourth commandment when I take my piddling vacation every year or call in sick during the week?

In the early 1980s, without a working permit, I used to hang wallpaper in Switzerland. On every job, we made an escape route so that if the authorities came, I could jump out a window or flee out a back door. But on Sundays, I didn't work at all because the Swiss were strict in enforcing Sunday laws, and those I worked with didn't want to explain me as well. Was I acknowledging the sovereignty of the beast by obeying the Sunday law?

Of course not. Couldn't we, then, rest on Sunday, and even go to church if compelled? What's compromised by obeying a law that compels us to do what is not itself sinful? What Adventist hasn't gone to church on Sunday, either with family or friends, long after understanding its anti-Christian origin?

"Whenever it is possible," wrote Ellen White, "let religious services be held on Sunday. Make these meetings intensely interesting. Sing genuine revival hymns, and speak with power and assurance of the Saviour's love."[2] We break no commands by obeying Sunday laws or even by going to church on Sunday.

But what about those whose businesses necessitate being open six days a week? If God's commandment closes them on Sabbath, and human's on Sunday, a conflict occurs. Adventist problems with Sunday laws have centered around making ends meet, not getting the mark of the beast.

Arguing that Sunday laws were unjust, unconstitutional, and a slap at the authority of God, A. T. Jones advocated that members defy them in California. Ellen White rejected that position.

> To defy the Sunday laws will but strengthen in their persecution the religious zealots who are seeking to enforce them. Give them no occasion to call you lawbreakers. . . . One does not receive the mark of the beast because he shows that he realizes the wisdom of keeping the peace by refraining from work that gives offense. . . .
>
> The law for the observance of the first day of the week is the production of an apostate Christendom. Sunday is a child of the papacy, exalted by the Christian world above the sacred day of God's rest. In no case are God's people to pay it homage. But I wish them to understand that they are not doing God's will by braving opposition when He wishes them to avoid it. Thus they create prejudice so bitter that it is impossible for the truth to be proclaimed. Make no demonstration on Sunday in defiance of the law.[3]

"In no case" are God's people to pay homage to Sunday, yet they can refrain from work and even hold church services that day?

The story of the three Hebrews affirms Ellen White's position. Though Daniel 3 never specifically says that Shadrach, Meshach, and Abednego stood before the gold image at Dura while everyone else bowed, Ellen White does. "In the midst of the worshiping multitude," she wrote, "there were three men who were firmly resolved not thus to dishonor the God of heaven."[4] The commandment forbids bowing to idols, not standing before them.

Also, the Bible never mentions that they would have to bow to the image, until after they gathered before it. The decree said only to come to the dedication, though—after having lived for years among the idolatry of the Babylonians—Shadrach, Meshach, and Abednego must have known what to expect. Nevertheless, they obeyed human law as far as they could without trampling God's, a precedent for Ellen White's position on obeying Sunday laws.

In contrast, when Daniel faced the decree forbidding prayer to anyone except Darius, he made no attempt to hide his worship. "Now when Daniel knew that the writing was signed, he went into his house; and his windows being open in his chamber toward Jerusalem, he kneeled upon his knees three times a day, and prayed, and gave thanks before his God, as he did aforetime" (Daniel 6:10).

Nothing in the Bible commanded that he pray with his window open, that he do it three times a day, or that he do it out loud. Could he not have hidden and still been faithful? Wasn't he inviting trouble, unlike his three compatriots, who acquiesced as far as possible? Didn't he openly defy the "Sunday law" of his time in a manner that Ellen White said to avoid?

One story seems to say, yield as far as possible; the other, don't give an inch.

Revelation warns against false worship: "If any man worship the beast and his image . . . the same shall drink of the wine of the wrath of God" (Revelation 14:9, 10). "They have no rest day nor night, who worship the beast and his image" (verse 11).

All this in contrast to the call to "worship him that made heaven, and earth, and the sea, and the fountains of waters" (Revelation 14:7).

If worship of the Creator involves obedience to the seventh-day Sabbath, then worshiping the beast will involve Sunday keeping. How far, then, can a Seventh-day Adventist go in obeying Sunday laws, even during the final conflict, without worshiping the beast? If we can refrain from work on Sunday, and even go to church, why should we be persecuted?

"Men will exalt and rigidly enforce," wrote Ellen White, "laws that are in direct opposition to the law of God. Though zealous in enforcing their own commandments, they will turn away from a plain 'Thus saith the Lord.' Exalting a spurious rest day, they will seek to force men to dishonor the law of Jehovah, the transcript of His character. . . . *The time is coming when God's people will feel the hand of persecution because they keep holy the seventh day*"[5] (italics supplied).

"In defiance of the warnings which God has given, they will continue *to trample upon one of the precepts of the Decalogue*, until they are led to persecute those who hold it sacred"[6] (italics supplied).

If the great controversy climaxes around God's law, then Sabbath, not Sunday, must be the central issue, because a person isn't violating God's law if he worships, or refrains from work, on the first day of the week. Violation comes only with transgression of the seventh.

Yet Ellen White writes that persecution will come also because of refusal to bow to Sunday. "[I]t will be declared that men are offending God *by violation of the Sunday sabbath*; that this sin has brought calamities which will not cease until Sunday observance shall be strictly enforced; and that those who present the claims of the fourth commandment, thus destroying reverence for Sunday, are troublers of the people, preventing their restoration to divine favor and temporal prosperity"[7](italics supplied).

"As the defenders of truth *refuse to honor the Sunday-sabbath*, some of them will be thrust into prison, some will be exiled, some will be treated as slaves"[8] (italics supplied).

"The powers of earth, uniting to war against the commandments of God, will decree that 'all, both small and great, rich and poor, free and bond' (Revelation 13:16), shall conform to the customs of the church by the observance of the false sabbath. *All who refuse compliance* will be visited with civil penalties, and it will finally be declared that they are deserving of death"[9] (italics supplied).

Does persecution come because we keep Sabbath or because we won't keep Sunday? If it's not sinful to refrain from work on Sunday, why should anyone be persecuted for keeping Sabbath?

"All who will not bow to the decree of the national councils and obey the national laws to exalt the sabbath instituted by the man of sin, *to the disregard of God's holy day*, will feel, not the oppressive power of popery alone, but of the Protestant world, the image of the beast"[10](italics supplied).

"With the issue thus clearly brought before him, whoever *shall trample upon God's law to obey a human enactment* receives the mark of the beast; he accepts the sign of allegiance to the power which he chooses to obey instead of God"[11] (italics supplied).

Why would "obeying a human enactment" automatically make us "trample upon God's law"? Adventists have obeyed Sunday laws for years, often at an economic expense, without violating the fourth commandment. Ellen White writes that we will be pushed to "honor the Sunday."[12] Is refraining from work, or even going to church, honoring "the Sunday"? If that's all that's involved, shouldn't we obey?

"As the Sabbath has become the special point of controversy throughout Christendom, and religious and secular authorities have combined to enforce the observance of the Sunday, the *persistent refusal of a small minority to yield to the popular demand* will make them objects of universal execration"[13] (italics supplied).

Perhaps, under the unique circumstances of the final days, we will not even make a pretense of obeying Sunday laws; instead, like Daniel, we might openly defy them. Or, like the three Hebrews, our acquiescence won't be any more acceptable to our persecutors than their acquiescence was to theirs. We might be pressured, not only to obey, but to profess allegiance to Sunday, as opposed to Sabbath, something that God's faithful people—who keep all the commandments—won't do.

However much the issue of Sunday observance factors in, Sabbath, not Sunday, must be the rub, the crucial issue for the faithful remnant, who "keep the commandments of God, and the faith of Jesus" (Revelation 14:12). If we were forced to refrain from work on the third, sixth, or fifth day, not the first, it wouldn't matter. What matters is what happens on Sabbath, not Sunday.

Whatever way the factors regarding the Sabbath controversy unfold, one thing's certain: whether like Daniel, and not giving in an inch, or like the three Hebrews, and acquiescing to a degree—anyone who remains faithful will need, not just knowledge of the Sabbath, but the *experience* as well.

---

1. Raoul Dederen, "Refelctions on a Theology of the Sabbath," in *The Sabbath in Scripture and History*, edited by Kenneth Strand (Hagerstown, Md.: Review and Herald Publishing Assn., 1982), 302.
2. *Testimonies for the Church*, 9:233.
3. Ibid., 232, 235.
4. Ellen G. White, *Prophets and Kings* (Boise, Idaho: Pacific Press Publishing Assn, 1943), 506.
5. *Testimonies for the Church*, 9:229.
6. *The Great Controversy*, 603.
7. Ibid., 590.
8. Ibid., 608.
9. Ibid., 604.
10. *Selected Messages*, 2:380.
11. *The Great Controversy*, 604.
12. Ibid., 592.
13. Ibid., 615.

CHAPTER
TWELVE

"[A]nd if they turn back from the faith, take them, and kill them, wherever ye find them" (Koran).

"The Toleration of those that differ from others in Matters of Religion, is so agreeable to the Gospel of Jesus Christ, and to the genuine Reason of Mankind, that it seems monstrous for Men to be so blind, as not to perceive the Necessity and Advantage of it" (John Locke, *A Letter Concerning Toleration*, 25).

"It may not be easy, in every possible case, to trace the line of separation between the rights of religion and the Civil authority with such distinctness as to avoid collisions & doubts" (James Madison, quoted by John F. Wilson, *Church and State in American History*, 40).

One of the worst treatises by a Seventh-day Adventist on religious liberty was *Christian Patriotism*, written by A. T. Jones in 1900.[1] However eloquent Jones's testimony was before the U.S. Senate twelve years earlier, *Christian Patriotism* exemplified the uncompromising extremism of his later years, an unbending dogmatism that ultimately led him out of the church.[2] Jones's reasoning throughout *Christian Patriotism* was *argumentum ad absurdio*.

"Separation of religion and the State," he wrote in the early pages, "is one of the original thoughts of the Bible, and reaches from the beginning to the end of the Book."[3]

Next, Jones contended that if man had never sinned, there never would have been a state, and thus religion would have never been united to it (you can't unite with what doesn't exist). "We have seen that such a condition maintained from the beginning would have been the absolute separation of religion and the State; because, then, there never could have been any State."[3]

But man did sin, and because Christianity is to restore man to his original condition, Jones wrote, "It follows with perfect conclusiveness that Christianity in its very essence, from the beginning to the end, and everywhere, demands the absolute separation of religion and the State in all who profess it" (ibid.).

Jones then cited various "biblical" examples of the absolute separation of religion from the state: "In thus separating Abraham from that State, from his country, God taught the people then, and through all time, the separation of religion and the State, the separation of Church and State" (ibid., 17).

"God's people must be called out of Egypt, in order that they and all the nations might be instructed in the great principles of the Gospel, of supreme allegiance to God, of the separation of religion and the State, of church and country" (ibid., 25).

According to Jones, when God called Israel to be His peculiar people, He "intended to teach them and all people forever that His plainly-declared will is that there shall be a complete separation between His church and every State or kingdom on the earth; that there shall never be any connection between His religion and any State or kingdom in the world" (ibid., 32, 33).

Jones claimed that Christ's words about rendering to Caesar his things and to God His "taught as plainly as it is possible to do, the complete separation of religion and the State" (ibid., 64).

These points vary from weak to absurd.

First, his claim that separation of religion and the state is a thought that "reaches from the beginning to the end of the Book [the Bible]" exemplifies Jones's extremism. The *principle* behind separation of church and state—i.e., freedom of conscience—is found in Scripture, particularly in the life and teaching of Jesus, but separation of church and state as such is not a theme running from Genesis to Revelation, nor is it "one of the leading principles of that Book" (ibid., 4). On the contrary, most of the Bible—especially the Old Testament—never even remotely deals with the subject.

Second, Jones's major premise, that before sin entered, religion and the state were completely separate because there was no state, is an abstract deduction about a time and environment—the world before sin—that we can only speculate on. You could just as easily argue that before sin there was no separation whatsoever. Everything was directly under the control of God's government. Though Jones tried to distinguish between a "society" and a "state" and say that before sin there was a society, as opposed to a state, the distinction is irrelevant: whatever it was, society or state, it was under God's control. Call it whatever you want, but it's not separation.

Then, even if this premise were correct, he reasoned it to an absurd extreme. Taking his same argument, we could argue that because Adam and Eve were originally created naked, "Christianity in its very essence, from the beginning to the end, and everywhere, demands that Christians go around in their birthday suits."

Meanwhile, getting separation of church and state from God's calling Abraham out of Ur of the Chaldees (and the Jews out of Egypt) is like getting the right to a jury trial from Christ's words, "Where two or three come together in my name, there am I with them" (Matthew 18:20, NIV).

Jones asserted that Israel has been made a distinct entity in order to teach the world that "there shall never be any connection between His religion and any State or kingdom in the world." God wanted Israel separate from the world, true, but not as an end in itself; instead, this separation was for the purpose of evangelization: Israel was to stay pure in order to be used by God to reach the heathen. This has nothing to do with separation of church and state. If anything, the theocracy of ancient Israel—where civil and religious laws were inseparable—made that nation a poor example of the separation principle.

Finally, Jones claimed that Christ's words about rendering to God and to Caesar "taught as plainly as it is possible to do, the complete separation of religion and the State." Possibly, but not necessarily. Christ's answer, more than likely, simply acknowledged that we should give to the government its service and to God His. No doubt, Jesus affirms the difference between the sphere of government and the sphere of God, but He doesn't say much more than that. Though the quote can be used to buttress the separation argument, Jones was recklessly dogmatic to assert that it teaches the "complete separation of church and state."

Yet Jones's positions lead to a bigger issue. His understanding of the Bible, his own Protestant theology, mandated that government be completely separate from religion; yet this premise itself *is religious*. For Jones, absolute separation of church and state, which means that religion should not be a part of government at all, originated from a religious perspective. By implementing absolute separation of church and state, then, the government centers a policy on the Bible itself, something which—according to Jones—the Bible forbids.

Besides, why should separationist theology be implemented in contrast to, say, Christian Reconstructionism, which believes that government should be completely united with religion, as in the Old Testament? The Reconstructionist position is as much a part of their theology as Jones's views on separation were his. The fact that Jones's theology was closer to the truth than the Reconstructionist's is irrelevant: our government shouldn't be basing policy on theology at all, whether correct or incorrect. (Of course, that last statement itself is based on a separationist theology; Reconstructionist theology would take a different view.)

In one sense, the Reconstructionist's position is less self-contradictory than Jones's, which mandates that government be completely separate from theology, yet bases that premise on theology. How could the government be separate from religion, when religion is the reason behind separation? The mere act of separating government from religion is, itself, an action based on theology.

Meanwhile, some Christians reject religious freedom outright. There is only one truth, one God, and only one way to worship that God, so why should people be allowed to follow and promote error? If "righteousness exalteth the nation" and sin brings the reproach of God, wouldn't it be in the best interests of the nation as a whole to force unanimity? However egregious, this view of religious freedom is just as much based on theology as was Jones's.

Then, too, if theology is behind the principle regarding the relationship between the church and the state, why should it be limited to Christian theology? Why not Muslim or Buddhist or Jewish theology instead?

As a church, we haven't adopted Jones's extremism, yet our separationism is rooted in theology as well: "That God as the Creator of all things has established the relationships that should prevail between Himself and humanity. . . . That God endowed humanity with intelligence. . . . That the church is a divinely ordained institution. . . . That humanity's two-fold duty to God and to government implies that God has delegated authority over strictly temporal matters to government, while reserving to Himself authority over strictly spiritual matters."[5]

We face the same conundrum as Jones's, if not to the same extent because we don't take it to the same extreme. Nevertheless, if our separationism derives from our theology and we try to push separationism on the government, are we not then actually trying to promote a public policy based specifically on theology, something that we decry in the New Right? Does the very implementation of the principle actually violate the principle itself?

Of course, strong secular arguments for separationism exist. Madalyn Murray O'Hair, the Ayatollah Khomeini of American atheism, doesn't work from a religious premise, nor do the American Civil Liberties Union, Americans United for Separation of Church and State, or many other organizations fighting for separationism.

"The two of them," wrote philosopher Immanuel Kant (hardly an orthodox Christian), "Church and State, ought to leave each other alone; they have no business interfering with one another."[6]

The American experiment in church-state separation has worked incredibly well for the church, which fact alone could justify separationism, apart from any religious considerations. On the other hand, in some countries where separation of church and state isn't implemented, the church is doing just fine, thank you. Plus, with America having the highest divorce rate in the world, with tens of thousands of murders annually, with billions of dollars spent on illicit drugs each year, with the largest prison population per capita in the world, with thousands of abortions per day, with an estimated one hundred thousand schoolchildren carrying guns to class, some could argue (as many erroneously do) that separation isn't so good after all.

"The United States boasts of its religious freedom and separation of church and state," wrote attorney John E. Stumbo. "Indeed, we recommend our church/state 'solution' to other societies experiencing religious conflict. But some of those societies look at our crime rates, sexual promiscuity and public secularism and say, 'Thanks, but no thanks.' "[7]

Prophecy does teach that America will be the great religious persecutor in the last days. Though this persecution comes only after America *repudiates* church-state separation, could one argue, in a classic Hegelian fashion, that the rampant freedom spawned by church-state separation will inevitably cause the backlash that makes America speak like a dragon?

Even if separationism is justified by totally secular reasoning, the concept itself—as formulated by America's founders—is rooted in theology.

Thomas Jefferson's famous "Bill for Establishing Religious Freedom" (Bill 82), long heralded as a precursor to church-state separation, began: "Almighty God hath created the mind free. . . ." Madison's famous "Memorial and Remonstrance" against a bill that would collect a tax for churches (another precursor to American separationism) used religious arguments as well: "If this freedom be abused, it is an offense against God, not against man: To God, therefore, and not Man, must an account be rendered."

Roger Williams, in many ways the founder of religious freedom on American soil and the one who coined the phrase "wall of separation," was a dogmatic Puritan who derived his religious liberty positions from theology.

Even British empiricist John Locke, whose writings profoundly influenced Thomas Jefferson's views on religious freedom, worked from a theological premise. "The care of Souls," Locke wrote in his classic *Letter Concerning Toleration*, "cannot belong to the Civil Magistrate, because his Power consists only in outward force; but true and saving Religion consists in the inward perswasion [sic] of the Mind, without which nothing can be acceptable to God. . . . I may grow rich by an Art that I take not delight in; I may be cured of some Disease by Remedies that I have not Faith in; but I cannot be saved by a Religion that I distrust, and by a Worship that I abhor."[8]

Thus, to be consistent with church-state separation principles, should church-state separation be abolished? Of course not! Though separationism in its earliest stages might have been rooted in religion—many valid secular reasons exist for its implementation today (the same argument is used, of course, to uphold Sunday laws).

An answer to this problem exists, though it does create more, possibly even worse, ones. In *The Great Controversy*, Ellen White wrote that in America "Republicanism and *Protestantism* became the fundamental principles of the nation. These principles are the secret of its power and prosperity"[9] (italics supplied).

By referring to Protestantism as one of America's two basic principles, Ellen White eradicated the conundrum regarding the implementation of church-state separation as a violation of the principle: separation is a Protestant principle (at least according to some Protestants), and because this country is based on Protestant principles, separationism is valid.

Though Ellen White never advocated enforcement of Protestant tenets in civil law, the claim that Protestantism is one of America's fundamental principles, even the secret of its prosperity, doesn't reflect church-state separationism, at least as it has been understood by the courts in the past fifty years. The statement sounds like Jerry Falwell and Pat Robertson, who argue that America must return to its "Christian" as opposed to "Protestant" (they can't offend their Roman Catholic allies) principles.

But what specific Protestant principles are the source of our prosperity, those of the Reverend Jerry Falwell or the Reverend Jesse Jackson? Should Protestant principles even be the basis of a nation with millions of Catholics, Jews, Muslims, Hindus, New Agers, and atheists? Do we really have a "wall of separation" if the state is founded on Protestantism, in any form?

Interestingly enough, Ellen White wrote that statement just after a period called "The Era of Protestant Republicanism"[10] in American history. Yet if any legislator today tried to pass a law openly based on "Protestant" principles, it would be attacked, and rightly so, as a violation of the Constitution. The Supreme Court in *Wallace v. Jaffree* struck down "a moment of silence" law for public schools because the language of the law might "endorse" voluntary prayer. That might be republicanism, but it sure *ain't* Protestantism.

In 1893, when A. T. Jones challenged devotional readings of the King James Bible in public schools, a thoroughly Protestant exercise (objection of some Catholics to the KJV readings in public school in earlier decades led to anti-Catholic riots in American streets), Ellen White told him to back off. "While I don't see the justice nor right in enforcing by law the bringing of the Bible to be read in public school, yet there are some things which burden my mind in regard to our people making prominent their ideas on this point."[11]

Apparently, her concern about the church's public image outweighed her concern about any constitutional infringement caused by the devotional exercises. This is not strict separationism, especially since the U.S. Supreme Court in 1963 ruled official Bible devotions in public schools unconstitutional.[12] Ellen White did write in an environment much more culturally, socially, and religiously homogenous than in 1963, a reality that no doubt influenced her views; but whatever the background, that law still subjected non-Protestants in public schools to the type of coercion the U.S. Supreme Court has repeatedly ruled unconstitutional.

In 1893, when Cecil Rhodes offered Adventists, at no cost, twelve thousand acres for a mission station, Jones called the gift a violation of church-state separation. Ellen White disagreed, telling the church, "What they would give we should be privileged to receive."[13] The Seventh-day Adventist Church in the United States, meanwhile, now struggles with the question of whether educational vouchers paid to parents of children who attend our schools violates church-state separation principles; on the other hand, in one part of Canada, the Adventist Church is *resisting* efforts by their government to terminate money that flows directly to the Adventist schools themselves!

Finally, Ellen White urged Adventists to work with the Women's Christian Temperance Union (WCTU), sort of the New Right of its day, particularly in support of the WCTU's effort to infringe upon the rights of consenting adults to drink alcoholic beverages, even in the privacy of their own homes. Again, contra Jones, she urged Adventists to continue cooperating with the WCTU on the temperance issue—even after the WCTU began advocating Sunday laws (something that the New Right today hasn't even yet done)!

What, then, is the solution? How does some poor Adventist— living in the last days, facing religious persecution—answer all the complicated questions about church-state separation? How does a church member—particularly one who hasn't read the *Federalist Papers* or *McGowan v. Maryland*—prepare herself for the arguments? If the greatest legal minds in America don't agree on almost any church-state controversy (as proven by the split decisions and rancorous debate of the Supreme Court), how can some loyal Adventist, wanting to stay faithful amid the coming crisis, understand all the hopelessly convoluted matters?

The answer is easy: She doesn't have to! The issue for those who "keep the commandments of God and have the faith of Jesus" (Revelation 14:12) isn't Ellen White and the WCTU or Thomas Jefferson's Sabbath-breaker bill or emergency powers acts; the issue is, simply—"the commandments of God and the faith of Jesus." However important for the church to defend separation of church and state now, the bottom line for God's faithful remnant isn't politics, jurisprudence, or constitutional law, but a saving relationship with Jesus Christ and the response that produces in our lives.

James Madison and Thomas Jefferson didn't die for our sins.

The Constitution isn't the Bible. Separation of church and state isn't the moral equivalent of justification by faith. And the eminences on the Supreme Court aren't the Holy Spirit. So, in the end, the crucial factors aren't the *Lemon* test, selective incorporation, or Earl Warren. The crucial factor is salvation in Jesus; it is not the First Amendment.

It's crucial to remember, too, that many Adventists—more than likely the majority—will face the mark of the beast in nations where the distinctive questions of the American experiment in religious freedom, such as separation of church and state, have never been factors. The universal issues involved in the final crisis between Christ and Satan—the character of God, the fairness of His law—transcend American constitutionalism, history, and church-state separation. Whatever the importance of these factors now, at least in the United States context, they will fade into insignificance as the great controversy climaxes. Article 1, Section 7's subtle acknowledgment of Sunday will hardly seem relevant in contrast to the cosmic struggles that have enthralled "the principalities and powers in heavenly places" (Ephesians 3:10) since Lucifer's rebellion.

Ultimately, for God's people, it doesn't matter what James Madison said or did or what the Fourteenth Amendment meant or how the Supreme Court rules on free-exercise cases. The faithful will stand on "the Bible, and the Bible only, as the standard of all doctrines and the basis of all reforms,"[14] not "the Constitution, and the Constitution only," because the Bible, not the Constitution, is our spiritual charter—and, at the core, the struggle is spiritual.

Whatever the importance of our understanding religious-liberty questions now, particularly in the realm of church-state separation, and however crucial for Adventists to stand behind their religious-liberty leaders during this struggle—in the final crunch, we can't lean on James Madison, the Constitution, or American history to defend our positions, because neither Madison, the Constitution, nor American history always do. When the world will be arrayed against us, we must trust only in what we're certain of, and that's the Bible—not the founding fathers, the First Amendment, or the Religious Freedom Restoration Act.

For God's commandment-keeping people, what matters most is God's law, not human's. Paul, though admonishing obedience to secular authorities, did sometimes write, after all, from jail—which shows that even obedience to political authorities has limits. As Peter said, "We ought to obey God rather than men" (Acts 5:29)—the defining principle for all who face end-time persecution.

Of course, Jehovah's Witnesses have been jailed, beaten, even killed because—by refusing to join the military, salute a flag, or sign an oath—they believed they were obeying God rather than humans. Catholics have been burned at the stake—refusing to give allegiance to anyone but the pope—believing they were obeying God, not people. How many Christians have been persecuted, obeying "God rather than men," by refusing to accept the Trinity and/or the deity of Christ, or, in the former Communist regimes, for refusing to violate the "Lord's day"?

Obviously, dying for a cause doesn't automatically make one righteous or the cause just. Millions of fanatics, or simply deceived souls, have given their lives for beliefs that had no sanction from the Word of God. The Lord is seeking faithful Christians who love and obey Him, not bodies to be burned because of false doctrines.

How, then, can we be sure that when persecuted, we'll be suffering for truth and not for error, like so many martyrs before us?

This, too, is easy. You don't need a Ph.D., an M.Div., or even a high-school education to understand "the commandments of God and the faith of Jesus" (Revelation 14:12).

The remnant aren't depicted as those who know the 2300 days, the state of the dead, and the Spirit of Prophecy (though all these elements will make it easier to be among that final remnant). Instead, two elements alone—faith and law—the essentials of true Christianity, constitute the distinguishing marks of God's final generation.

And even these can be narrowed somewhat. Unlike George Orwell's nightmare utopia *1984*, where "thoughtcrime" was punished, the struggle with the state won't even be over the "faith of Jesus," but with "the commandments of God." The government can't do much about the first part (after all, according to prophecy, we will be persecuted by those who themselves profess the faith of Jesus), but it can with the second, which is why a Christian needs to know exactly what "the commandments of God" are and why she needs to follow them. Whatever laws human rulers might make against the commandments of God, no law can touch the "faith of Jesus," and it's that faith which gives God's people the power, motive, and courage to keep His commandments.

Though the present truths of Adventism facilitate preparation for the final struggle between Christ and Satan, the real battle deals, not with basic Adventism, but with basic Christianity—and what's more basic than the "commandments of God"? And, especially as experience can show, what's more basic to the commandments than the Sabbath?

The bottom line? Though our theological base is as firm as "the commandments of God and the faith of Jesus," our political one is shaky. However lofty and divine the principles behind them, our rights, freedoms, and privileges are made real only through imperfect documents, written and interpreted by sinful and imperfect humans who enforce them through imperfect, even corrupt institutions—which is why, in the end, we can't trust them.

The Constitution of the United States sits in a glass case displayed in the Archives in downtown Washington, D.C. The document itself is faded, hard to read. The same with the Bill of Rights, ensconced in a case next to the Constitution. Eventually, the words of both will diminish beyond readability. That says something, but only those with an understanding of America's prophetic role can truly hear what.

"The Constitution," wrote Ellen White, "provides that 'Congress shall make no law respecting an establishment of religion, or prohibiting the free exercise thereof. . . .' Only in flagrant violation of these safeguards to the nation's liberty, can any religious observance be enforced by civil authority. But the inconsistency of such action is no greater than is represented by the symbol. It is the beast with lamblike horns—in profession pure, gentle, and harmless—that speaks as a dragon."[15]

We warn, we cajole, we fight, but—in the political arena—we lose. Fortunately, the battle is spiritual, for "we wrestle not against flesh and blood, but against principalities, against powers, against the rulers of the darkness of this world" (Ephesians 6:12) and—through a born-again experience, partaking of the victory that Jesus won for us—we can be assured of success, whatever the fate of our freedoms.

---

1. A. T. Jones, *Christian Patriotism or Religion and the State* (Boise, Idaho: Pacific Press Publishing Assn., 1900).

2. George Knight, *From 1888 to Apostasy* (Hagerstown, Md.: Review and Herald Publishing Association, 1989).

3. *Christian Patriotism or Religion and the State*, 5.

4. Ibid., 5.

5. North American Division of the General Conference, *Working Policy* HC O5 02, 247, 248

6. Quoted in Franz Wiedmann, *Hegel* (New York: Pegasus, 1968), 29.

7. John E. Stumbo, "Stopping the Drift Toward Moral Chaos," *News Network International*, 21 April 1995.

8. John Locke, in *Letter Concerning Toleration*, edited by Jamto Trulley (Indianapolis, Ind.: Hackett Publishing Company, Inc., 1983), 27, 38.

9. *The Great Controvery*, 441.

10. See John E. Wilson and Donald L. Drakeman, *Church and State in American History* (Boston: Beacon Press, 1987).

11. Ellen G. White, letter 44, 1893.

12. *Abington v. Schempp.*

13. Ellen G. White, *Testimonies to Ministers* (Boise, Idaho: Pacific Press Publishing Assn., 1962), 197.

14. *The Great Controversy*, 595.

15. Ibid., 442.

APPENDIX

Evangelicals and Catholics Together: The Christian Mission in the Third Millennium

The following statement is the product of consultation, beginning in September 1992, between Evangelical Protestant and Roman Catholic Christians. Appended to the text is a list of participants in the consultation and of others who have given their support to this declaration.

Introduction

1. We are Evangelical Protestant and Roman Catholics who have been led through prayer, study, and discussion to common convictions about Christian faith and mission. This statement cannot speak officially for our communities. It does intend to speak responsibly from our communities and to our communities. In this statement we address what we have discovered both about our unity and about our differences. We are aware that our experience reflects the distinctive circumstances and opportunities of Evangelicals and Catholics living together in North America. At the same time, we believe that what we have discovered and resolved is pertinent to the relationship between Evangelicals and Catholics in other parts of the world. We therefore commend this statement to their prayerful consideration.

2. As the Second Millennium draws to a close, the Christian mission in world history faces a moment of daunting opportunity and responsibility. If in the merciful and mysterious ways of God the Second Coming is delayed, we enter upon a Third Millennium that could be, in the words of John Paul II, "a springtime of world missions." (*Redemptoris Missio*)

3. As Christ is one, so the Christian mission is one. That one mission can be and should be advanced in diverse ways. Legitimate diversity, however, should not be confused with existing divisions between Christians that obscure the one Christ and hinder the one mission. There is a necessary connection between the visible unity of Christians and the mission of the one Christ. We together pray for the fulfillment of the prayer of Our Lord: "May they all be one; as you, Father, are in me and I in you, so also may they be in us, that the world may believe that you sent me." (John 17) We together, Evangelicals and Catholics, confess our sins against the unity that Christ intends for all his disciples.

4. The one Christ and one mission includes many other Christians, notably the Eastern Orthodox and those Protestants not commonly identified as Evangelical. All Christians are encompassed in the prayer, "May they all be one." Our present statement attends to the specific problems and opportunities in the relationship between Roman Catholics and Evangelical Protestants.

5. As we near the Third Millennium, there are approximately 1.7 billion Christians in the world. About a billion of these are Catholics and more than 300 million are Evangelical Protestants. The century now drawing to a close has been the greatest century of missionary expansion in Christian history. We pray and we believe that this expansion has prepared the way for yet greater missionary endeavor in the first century of the Third Millennium.

6. The two communities in world Christianity that are most evangelistically assertive and most rapidly growing are Evangelicals and Catholics. In many parts of the world, the relationship between these communities is marked more by conflict than by cooperation, more by animosity than by love, more by suspicion than by trust, more by propaganda and ignorance than by respect for the truth. This is alarmingly the case in Latin America, increasingly the case in Eastern Europe, and too often the case in our own country.

7. Without ignoring conflicts between and within other Christian communities, we address ourselves to the relationship between Evangelicals and Catholics, who constitute the growing edge of missionary expan-

sion at present and, most likely, in the century ahead. In doing so, we hope that what we have discovered and resolved may be of help in other situations of conflict, such as that among Orthodox, Evangelicals, and Catholics in Eastern Europe. While we are gratefully aware of ongoing efforts to address tensions among these communities, the shameful reality is that, in many places around the world, the scandal of conflict between Christians obscures the scandal of the cross, thus crippling the one mission of the one Christ.

8. As in times past, so also today and in the future, the Christian mission, which is directed to the entire human community, must be advanced against formidable opposition. In some cultures, that mission encounters resurgent spiritualities and religions that are explicitly hostile to the claims of the Christ. Islam, which in many instances denies the freedom to witness to the Gospel, must be of increasing concern to those who care about religious freedom and the Christian mission. Mutually respectful conversation between Muslims and Christians should be encouraged in the hope that more of the world will, in the oft-repeated words of John Paul II, "open the door to Christ." At the same time, in our so-called developed societies, a widespread secularization increasingly descends into moral, intellectual, and spiritual nihilism that denies not only the One who is the Truth but the very idea of truth itself.

9. We enter the twenty-first century without illusions. With Paul and the Christians of the first century, we know that "we are not contending against flesh and blood, but against the principalities, against the powers, against the world rulers of this present darkness, against the spiritual hosts of wickedness in the heavenly places." (Ephesians 6) As Evangelicals and Catholics, we dare not by needless and loveless conflict between ourselves give aid and comfort to the enemies of the cause of Christ.

10. The love of Christ compels us and we are therefore resolved to avoid such conflict between our communities and, where such conflict exists, to do what we can to reduce and eliminate it. Beyond that, we are called and we are therefore resolved to explore patterns of working and witnessing together in order to advance the one mission of Christ. Our common resolve is not based merely on a desire for harmony. We reject any appearance of harmony that is purchased at the price of truth. Our common resolve is made imperative by obedience of the truth of God revealed in the Word of God, the Holy Scriptures, and by the trust in the promise of the Holy Spirit's guidance until Our

Lord returns in glory to judge the living and the dead.

The mission that we embrace together is the necessary consequence of the faith that we affirm together.

We Affirm Together

11. Jesus Christ is Lord. That is the first and final affirmation that Christians make about all of reality. He is the One sent by God to be Lord
and Savior of all: "And there is salvation in no one else, for there is no
other name under heaven given among men by which we must be
saved." (Acts 4) Christians are people ahead of time, those who proclaim now what will one day be acknowledged by all, that Jesus Christ
is Lord. (Philippians 2)

12. We affirm together that we are justified by grace through faith because of Christ. Living faith is active in love that is nothing less than
the love of Christ, for we together say with Paul: "I have been crucified with Christ; it is no longer I who live, but Christ who lives in me;
and the life I now live in the flesh I live by faith in the Son of God,
who loved me and gave himself for me." (Galatians 2)

13. All who accept Christ as Lord and Savior are brothers and sisters in
Christ. Evangelicals and Catholics are brothers and sisters in Christ.
We have not chosen one another, just as we have not chosen Christ.
He has chosen us, and he has chosen us to be his together. (John 15)
However imperfect our communion with one another, however deep
our disagreements with one another, we recognize that there is but
one church of Christ. There is one church because there is one Christ
and the church is his body. However difficult the way, we recognize
that we are called by God to a fuller realization of our unity in the
body of Christ. The only unity to which we would give expression is
unity in the truth, and the truth is this: "There is one body and one
Spirit, just as you were called to the one hope that belongs to your
call, one Lord, one faith, one baptism, one God and father of us all,
who is above all and through all and in all." (Ephesians 4)

14. We affirm together that Christians are to teach and live in obedience
to the divinely inspired Scriptures, which are the infallible Word of
God. We further affirm together that Christ has promised to his church
the gift of the Holy Spirit who will lead us into all truth in discerning
and declaring the teaching of Scripture. (John 16) We recognize together that the Holy Spirit has so guided his church in the past. In, for
instance, the formation of the canon of the Scriptures, and in the orthodox response to the great Christological and Trinitarian contro-

versies of the early centuries, we confidently acknowledge the guidance of the Holy Spirit. In faithful response to the Spirit's leading, the church formulated the Apostles' Creed, which we can and hereby do affirm together as an accurate statement of scriptural truth:

I believe in God, the Father almighty, creator of heaven and earth.

I believe in Jesus Christ, his only Son, our Lord. He was conceived by the power of the Holy Spirit and born of the virgin Mary. He suffered under Pontius Pilate, was crucified, died and was buried. He descended into hell. On the third day he rose again. He ascended into heaven, and is seated at the right hand of the Father. He will come again to judge the living and the dead.

I believe in the Holy Spirit, the holy catholic Church, the communion of saints, the forgiveness of sins, the resurrection of the body, and the life everlasting. Amen.

We Hope Together

15. We hope together that all people will come to faith in Jesus Christ as Lord and Savior. This hope makes necessary the church's missionary zeal. "But how are they to call upon him in whom they have not believed? And how are they to hear without a preacher? And how can men preach unless they are sent?" (Romans 10) The church is by nature, in all places and at all times, in mission. Our missionary hope is inspired by the revealed desire of God that "all should be saved and come to a knowledge of the truth." (1 Timothy 2)

16. The church lives by and for the Great Commission: "Go therefore and make disciples of all nations, baptizing them in the name of the Father and of the Son and of the Holy Spirit, teaching them to observe all that I have commanded you; and lo, I am with you always, to the close of the age." (Matthew 28)

17. Unity and love among Christians is an integral part of our missionary witness to the Lord whom we serve. "A new commandment I give to you, that you love one another; even as I have loved you, that you also love one another. By this all men will know that you are my disciples, if you have love for one another." (John 13) If we do not love one another, we disobey this command and contradict the Gospel we declare.

18. As Evangelicals and Catholics, we pray that our unity in the love of Christ will become ever more evident as a sign to the world of God's reconciling power. Our communal and ecclesial separations are deep

and long standing. We acknowledge that we do not know the schedule nor do we know the way to the greater visible unity for which we hope. We do know that existing patterns of distrustful polemic and conflict are not the way. We do know that God who has brought us into communion with himself through Christ intends that we also be in communion with one another. We do know that Christ is the way, the truth, and the life (John 14) and as we are drawn closer to him—walking in that way, obeying that truth, living that life—we are drawn closer to one another.

19. Whatever may be the future form of the relationship between our communities, we can, we must, and we will begin now the work required to remedy what we know to be wrong in that relationship. Such work requires trust and understanding, and trust and understanding require an assiduous attention to truth. We do not deny but clearly assert that there are disagreements between us. Misunderstandings, misrepresentations, and caricatures of one another, however, are not disagreements. These distortions must be cleared away if we are to search through our honest differences in a manner consistent with what we affirm and hope together on the basis of God's Word.

We Search Together

20. Together we search for a fuller and clearer understanding of God's revelation of Christ and his will for his disciples. Because of the limitations of human reason and language, which limitations are compounded by sin, we cannot understand completely the transcendent reality of God and his ways. Only in the End Time will we see face to face and know as we are known. (1 Corinthians 13) We now search together in confident reliance upon God's self-revelation in Jesus Christ, the sure testimony of Holy Scripture, and the promise of the Spirit to his church. In this search to understand the truth more fully and clearly, we need one another. We are both informed and limited by the histories of our communities and by our own experiences. Across the divides of communities and experiences, we need to challenge one another, always speaking the truth in love, building up the Body. (Ephesians 4)

21. We do not presume to suggest that we can resolve the deep and long-standing differences between Evangelicals and Catholics. Indeed these differences may never be resolved short of the Kingdom Come. Nonetheless, we are not permitted simply to resign ourselves to differences that divide us from one another. Not all differences are authentic dis-

agreements, nor need all disagreements divide. Differences and disagreements must be tested in disciplined and sustained conversation. In this connection we warmly commend and encourage the formal theological dialogues of recent years between Roman Catholics and Evangelicals.

22. We note some of the differences and disagreements that must be addressed more fully and candidly in order to strengthen between us a relationship of trust in obedience to truth. Among points of difference in doctrine, worship, practice, and piety that are frequently thought to divide us are these:

◆ The church as an integral part of the Gospel or the church as communal consequence of the Gospel.
◆ The church as visible communion or invisible fellowship of true believers.
◆ The sole authority of Scripture (*sola scriptura*) or Scripture as authoritatively interpreted in the church.
◆ The "soul freedom" of the individual Christian or the Magisterium (teaching authority) of the community.
◆ The church as local congregation or universal communion.
◆ Ministry ordered in apostolic succession or the priesthood of all believers.
◆ Sacraments and ordinances as symbols of grace or means of grace.
◆ The Lord's Supper as eucharistic sacrifice or memorial meal.
◆ Remembrance of Mary and the saints or devotion to Mary and the saints.
◆ Baptism as sacrament of regeneration or testimony to regeneration.

23. This account of differences is by no means complete. Nor is the disparity between positions always so sharp as to warrant the "or" in the above formulations. Moreover, among those recognized as Evangelical Protestants there are significant differences between, for example, Baptists, Pentecostals, and Calvinists on these questions. But the differences mentioned above reflect disputes that are deep and long standing. In at least some instances, they reflect authentic disagreements that have been in the past and are at present barriers to full communion between Christians.

24. On these questions, and other questions implied by them, Evangelicals hold that the Catholic Church has gone beyond Scripture, adding teachings and practices that detract from or compromise the Gospel of God's saving grace in Christ. Catholics, in turn, hold that such teach-

ing and practices are grounded in Scripture and belong to the fullness of God's revelation. Their rejection, Catholics say, results in a truncated and reduced understanding of the Christian reality.

25. Again, we cannot resolve these disputes here. We can and do affirm together that the entirety of Christian faith, life, and mission finds its source, center, and end in the crucified and risen Lord. We can and do pledge that we will continue to search together—through study, discussion, and prayer—for a better understanding of one another's convictions and a more adequate comprehension of the truth of God in Christ. We can testify now that in our searching together we have discovered what we can affirm together and what we can hope together and, therefore, how we can contend together.

We Contend Together

26. As we are bound together by Christ and his cause, so we are bound together in contending against all that opposes Christ and his cause. We are emboldened not by illusions of easy triumph but by faith in his certain triumph. Our Lord wept over Jerusalem, and he now weeps over a world that does not know the time of its visitation. The raging of the principalities and powers may increase as the End Time nears, but the outcome of the contest is assured.

27. The cause of Christ is the cause and mission of the church, which is, first of all, to proclaim the Good News that "God was in Christ reconciling the world to himself, not counting their trespasses against them, and entrusting to us the message of reconciliation." (2 Corinthians 5) To proclaim this Gospel and to sustain the community of faith, worship, and discipleship that is gathered by this Gospel is the first and chief responsibility of the church. All other tasks and responsibilities of the church are derived from and directed toward the mission of the Gospel.

28. Christians individually and the church corporately also have a responsibility for the right ordering of civil society. We embrace this task soberly; knowing the consequences of human sinfulness, we resist the utopian conceit that it is within our powers to build the Kingdom of God on earth. We embrace this task hopefully; knowing that God has called us to love our neighbor, we seek to secure for all a greater measure of civil righteousness and justice, confident that he will crown our efforts when he rightly orders all things in the coming of his Kingdom.

29. In the exercise of these public responsibilities there has been in recent

years a growing convergence and cooperation between Evangelicals and Catholics. We thank God for the discovery of one another in contending for a common cause. Much more important, we thank God for the discovery of one another as brothers and sisters in Christ. Our cooperation as citizens is animated by our convergence as Christians. We promise one another that we will work to deepen, build upon, and expand this pattern of convergence and cooperation.

30. Together we contend for the truth that politics, law, and culture must be secured by moral truth. With the Founders of the American experiment, we declare, "We hold these truths." With them, we hold that this constitutional order is composed not just of rules and procedures but is most essentially a moral experiment. With them, we hold that only a virtuous people can be free and just, and that virtue is secured by religion. To propose that securing civil virtue is the purpose of religion is blasphemous. To deny that securing civil virtue is a benefit of religion is blindness.

31. Americans are drifting away from, are often explicitly defying the constituting truths of this experiment in ordered liberty. Influential sectors of the culture are laid waste by relativism, anti-intellectualism, and nihilism that deny the very idea of truth. Against such influences in both the elite and popular culture, we appeal to reason and religion in contending for the foundational truths of our constitutional order.

32. More specifically, we contend together for religious freedom. We do so for the sake of religion, but also because religious freedom is the first freedom, the source and shield of all human freedoms. In their relationship to God, persons have a dignity and responsibility that transcends, and thereby limits, the authority of the state and of every other merely human institution.

33. Religious freedom is itself grounded in and is a product of religious faith, as is evident in the history of Baptists and others in this country. Today we rejoice together that the Roman Catholic Church—as affirmed by the Second Vatican Council and boldly exemplified in the ministry of John Paul II—is strongly committed to religious freedom and, consequently, to the defense of all human rights. Where Evangelicals and Catholics are in severe and sometimes violent conflict, such as parts of Latin America, we urge Christians to embrace and act upon the imperative of religious freedom. Religious freedom will not be respected by the state if it is not respected by Christians or, even worse, if Christians attempt to recruit the state in repressing religious freedom.

34. In this country, too, freedom of religion cannot be taken for granted but requires constant attention. We strongly affirm the separation of church and state, and just as strongly protest the distortion of that principle to mean the separation of religion from public life. We are deeply concerned by the court's narrowing of the protections provided by the "free exercise" provision of the First Amendment and by an obsession with "no establishment" that stifles the necessary role of religion in American life. As a consequence of such distortions, it is increasingly the case that wherever government goes religion must retreat, and government increasingly goes almost everywhere. Religion, which was privileged and foundational in our legal order, has in recent years been penalized and made marginal. We contend together for a renewal of the constituting vision of the place of religion in the American experiment.

35. Religion and religiously grounded moral conviction is not an alien or threatening force in our public life. For the great majority of Americans, morality is derived, however variously and confusedly, from religion. The argument, increasingly voiced in sectors of our political culture, that religion should be excluded from the public square must be recognized as an assault upon the most elementary principles of democratic governance. That argument needs to be exposed and countered by leaders, religious and other, who care about the integrity of our constitutional order.

36. The pattern of convergence and cooperation between Evangelicals and Catholics is, in large part, a result of common effort to protect human life, especially the lives of the most vulnerable among us. With the Founders, we hold that all human beings are endowed by their Creator with the right to life, liberty, and the pursuit of happiness. The statement that the unborn child is a human life that—barring natural misfortune or lethal intervention—will become what everyone recognizes as a human baby is not a religious assertion. It is a statement of simple biological fact. That the unborn child has a right to protection, including the protection of law, is a moral statement supported by moral reason and biblical truth.

37. We, therefore, will persist in contending—we will not be discouraged but will multiply every effort—in order to secure the legal protection of the unborn. Our goals are: to secure due process of law for the unborn, to enact the most protective laws and public policies that are politically possible, and to reduce dramatically the incidence of abortion. We warmly commend those who have established thousands of

crisis pregnancy and postnatal care centers across the country, and urge that such efforts be multiplied. As the unborn must be protected, so also must women be protected from their current rampant exploitation by the abortion industry and by fathers who refuse to accept responsibility for mothers and children. Abortion on demand, which is the current rule in America, must be recognized as a massive attack on the dignity, rights, and needs of women.

38. Abortion is the leading edge of an encroaching culture of death. The helpless old, the radically handicapped, and others who cannot effectively assert their rights are increasingly treated as though they have no rights. These are the powerless who are exposed to the will and whim of those who have power over them. We will do all in our power to resist proposals for euthanasia, eugenics, and population control that exploit the vulnerable, corrupt the integrity of medicine, deprave our culture, and betray the moral truths of our constitutional order.

39. In public education, we contend together for schools that transmit to coming generations our cultural heritage which is inseparable from the formative influence of religion, especially Judaism and Christianity. Education for responsible citizenship and social behavior is inescapably moral education. Every effort must be made to cultivate the morality of honesty, law observance, work, caring, chastity, mutual respect between the sexes, and readiness for marriage, parenthood, and family. We reject the claim that, in any or all of these areas, "tolerance" requires the promotion of moral equivalence between the normative and the deviant. In a democratic society that recognizes that parents have the primary responsibility for the formation of their children, schools are to assist and support, not oppose and undermine, parents in the exercise of their responsibility.

40. We contend together for a comprehensive policy of parental choice in education. This is a moral question of simple justice. Parents are the primary educators of their children; the state and other institutions should be supportive of their exercise of the responsibility. We affirm policies that enable parents to effectively exercise their right and responsibility to choose the schooling that they consider best for their children.

41. We contend together against the widespread pornography in our society, along with the celebration of violence, sexual depravity, and antireligious bigotry in the entertainment media. In resisting such cultural and moral debasement, we recognize the legitimacy of boycotts and other consumer actions, and urge the enforcement of exist-

ing laws against obscenity. We reject the self-serving claim of the peddlers of depravity that this constitutes illegitimate censorship. We reject the assertion of the unimaginative that artistic creativity is to be measured by the capacity to shock or outrage. A people incapable of defending decency invites the rule of viciousness, both public and personal.

42. We contend for a renewed spirit of acceptance, understanding, and cooperation across lines of religion, race, ethnicity, sex, and class. We are all created in the image of God and are accountable to him. That truth is the basis of individual responsibility and equality before the law. The abandonment of that truth has resulted in a society at war with itself, pitting citizens against one another in bitter conflicts of group grievances and claims to entitlement. Justice and social amity require a redirection of public attitudes and policies so that rights are joined to duties and people are rewarded according to their character and competence.

43. We contend for a free society, including a vibrant market economy. A free society requires a careful balancing between economics, politics, and culture. Christianity is not an ideology and therefore does not prescribe precisely how that balance is to be achieved in every circumstance. We affirm the importance of a free economy not only because it is more efficient but because it accords with a Christian understanding of human freedom. Economic freedom, while subject to grave abuse, makes possible the patterns of creativity, cooperation, and accountability that contribute to the common good.

44. We contend together for a renewed appreciation of Western culture. In its history and missionary reach, Christianity engages all cultures while being captive to none. We are keenly aware of, and grateful for, the role of Christianity in shaping and sustaining the Western culture of which we are part. As with all of history, that culture is marred by human sinfulness. Alone among world cultures, however, the West has cultivated an attitude of self-criticism and of eagerness to learn from other cultures. What is called multiculturalism can mean respectful attention to human differences. More commonly today, however, multiculturalism means affirming all cultures but our own. Welcoming the contributions of other cultures and being ever alert to the limitations of our own, we receive Western culture as our legacy and embrace it as our task in order to transmit it as a gift to future generations.

45. We contend for public policies that demonstrate renewed respect for

the irreplaceable role of mediating structures in society—notably the family, churches, and myriad voluntary associations. The state is not the society, and many of the most important functions of society are best addressed in independence from the state. The role of churches in responding to a wide variety of human needs, especially among the poor and marginal, needs to be protected and strengthened. Moreover, society is not the aggregate of isolated individuals bearing rights but is composed of communities that inculcate responsibility, sustain shared memory, provide mutual aid, and nurture the habits that contribute to both personal well-being and the common good. Most basic among such communities is the community of the family. Laws and social policies should be designed with particular care for the stability and flourishing of families. While the crisis of the family in America is by no means limited to the poor or to the underclass, heightened attention must be paid those who have become, as a result of well-intended but misguided statist policies, virtual wards of the government.

46. Finally, we contend for a realistic and responsible understanding of America's part in world affairs. Realism and responsibility require that we avoid both the illusions of unlimited power and righteousness, on the one hand, and the timidity and selfishness of isolationism, on the other. U.S. foreign policy should reflect a concern for the defense of democracy and, wherever prudent and possible, the protection and advancement of human rights, including religious freedom.

47. The above is a partial list of public responsibilities on which we believe there is a pattern of convergence and cooperation between Evangelicals and Catholics. We reject the notion that this constitutes a partisan "religious agenda" in American politics. Rather, this is a set of directions oriented to the common good and discussable on the basis of public reason. While our sense of civic responsibility is informed and motivated by Christian faith, our intention is to elevate the level of political and moral discourse in a manner that excludes no one and invites the participation of all people of good will. To that end, Evangelicals and Catholics have made an inestimable contribution in the past and, it is our hope, will contribute even more effectively in the future.

48. We are profoundly aware that the American experiment has been, all in all, a blessing to the world and a blessing to us as Evangelical and Catholic Christians. We are determined to assume our full share of responsibility for this "one nation under God," believing

it to be a nation under the judgment, mercy, and providential care of the Lord of the nations to whom alone we render unqualified allegiance.

We Witness Together

49. The question of Christian witness unavoidably returns us to points of serious tension between Evangelicals and Catholics. Bearing witness to the saving power of Jesus Christ and his will for our lives is an integral part of Christian discipleship. The achievement of good will and cooperation between Evangelicals and Catholics must not be at the price of the urgency and clarity of Christian witness to the Gospel. At the same time, and as noted earlier, Our Lord has made clear that the evidence of love among his disciples is an integral part of that Christian witness.

50. Today, in this country and elsewhere, Evangelicals and Catholics attempt to win "converts" from one another's folds. In some ways, this is perfectly understandable and perhaps inevitable. In many instances, however, such efforts at recruitment undermine the Christian mission by which we are bound by God's Word and to which we have recommitted ourselves in this statement. It should be clearly understood between Catholics and Evangelicals that Christian witness is of necessity aimed at conversion. Authentic conversion is—in its beginning, in its end, and all along the way—conversion to God in Christ by the power of the Spirit. In this connection, we embrace as our own the explanation of the Baptist-Roman Catholic International Conversation (1988):

Conversion is turning away from all that is opposed to God, contrary to Christ's teaching, and turning to God, to Christ, the Son, through the work of the Holy Spirit. It entails a turning from the self-centeredness of sin to faith in Christ as Lord and Savior. Conversion is a passing from one way of life to another new one, marked with the newness of Christ. It is a continuing process so that the whole life of a Christian should be a passage from death to life, from error to truth, from sin to grace. Our life in Christ demands continual growth in God's grace. Conversion is personal but not private. Individuals respond in faith to God's call but faith comes from hearing the proclamation of the word of God and is to be expressed in the life together in Christ that is the Church.

51. By preaching, teaching, and life example, Christians witness to Christians and non-Christians alike. We seek and pray for the conversion of others, even as we recognize our own continuing need to be fully converted. As we strive to make Christian faith and life—our own and that of others—ever more intentional rather than nominal, ever more committed rather than apathetic, we also recognize the different forms that authentic discipleship can take. As is evident in the two thousand year history of the church, and in our contemporary experience, there are different ways of being Christian, and some of these ways are distinctively marked by communal patterns of worship, piety, and catechesis. That we are all to be one does not mean that we are all to be identical in our way of following the one Christ. Such distinctive patterns of discipleship, it should be noted, are amply evident within the communion of the Catholic Church as well as within the many worlds of Evangelical Protestantism.

52. It is understandable that Christians who bear witness to the Gospel try to persuade others that their communities and traditions are more fully in accord with the Gospel. There is a necessary distinction between evangelizing and what is today commonly called proselytizing or "sheep stealing." We condemn the practice of recruiting people from another community for purposes of denominational or institutional aggrandizement. At the same time, our commitment to full religious freedom compels us to defend the legal freedom to proselytize even as we call upon Christians to refrain from such activity.

53. Three observations are in order in connection with proselytizing. First, as much as we might believe one community is more fully in accord with the Gospel than another, we as Evangelicals and Catholics affirm that opportunity and means for growth in Christian discipleship are available in our several communities. Second, the decision of the committed Christian with respect to his communal allegiance and participation must be assiduously respected. Third, in view of the large number of non-Christians in the world and the enormous challenge of our common evangelistic task, it is neither theologically legitimate nor a prudent use of resources for one Christian community to proselytize among active adherents of another Christian community.

54. Christian witness must always be made in a spirit of love and humility. It must not deny but must readily accord to everyone the full freedom to discern and decide what is God's will for his life. Witness that is in service to the truth is in service to such freedom. Any form of coercion—physical, psychological, legal, economic—corrupts Christian

witness and is to be unqualifiedly rejected. Similarly, bearing false witness against other persons and communities, or casting unjust and uncharitable suspicions upon them, is incompatible with the Gospel. Also to be rejected is the practice of comparing the strengths and ideals of one community with the weaknesses and failures of another. In describing the teaching and practices of other Christians, we must strive to do so in a way that they would recognize as fair and accurate.

55. In considering the many corruptions of Christian witness, we, Evangelicals and Catholics, confess that we have sinned against one another and against God. We more earnestly ask the forgiveness of God and one another, and pray for the grace to amend our own lives and that of our communities.

56. Repentance and amendment of life do not dissolve remaining differences between us. In the context of evangelization and "reevangelization," we encounter a major difference in our understanding of the relationship between baptism and the new birth in Christ. For Catholics, all who are validly baptized are born again and are truly, however imperfectly, in communion with Christ. That baptismal grace is to be continually reawakened and revivified through conversion. For most Evangelicals, but not all, the experience of conversion is to be followed by baptism as a sign of the new birth. For Catholics, all the baptized are already members of the church, however dormant their faith and life; for many Evangelicals, the new birth requires baptismal initiation into the community of the born again. These differing beliefs about the relationship between baptism, new birth, and membership in the church should be honestly presented to the Christian who has undergone conversion. But again, his decision regarding communal allegiance and participation must be assiduously respected.

57. There are, then, differences between us that cannot be resolved here. But on this we are resolved: All authentic witness must be aimed at conversion to God in Christ by the power of the Holy Spirit. Those converted—whether understood as having received the new birth for the first time or as having experienced the reawakening of the new birth originally bestowed in the sacrament of baptism—must be given full freedom and respect as they discern and decide the community in which they will live their new life in Christ. In such discernment and decision, they are ultimately responsible to God and we dare not interfere with the exercise of that responsibility. Also in our differences and disagreements, we Evangelicals and Catholics commend one another to God "who by the power at work within us is able to do far

more abundantly than all that we ask or think" (Ephesians 3)

58. In this discussion of witnessing we have touched on difficult and long standing problems. The difficulties must not be permitted to over-shadow the truths on which we are, by the grace of God, in firm agreement. As we grow in mutual understanding and trust, it is our hope that our efforts to evangelize will not jeopardize but will reinforce our devotion to the common tasks to which we have pledged ourselves in this statement.

Conclusion

59. Nearly two thousand years after it began, and nearly five hundred years after the divisions of the Reformation era, the Christian mission to the world is vibrantly alive and assertive. We do not know, we cannot know, what the Lord of history has in store for the Third Millennium. It may be the springtime of world missions and great Christian expansion. It may be the way of the cross marked by persecution and apparent marginalization. In different places and times, it will likely be both. Or it may be that Our Lord will return tomorrow.

60. We do know that his promise is sure, that we are enlisted for the duration, and that we are in this together. We do know that we must affirm and hope and search and contend and witness together, for we belong not to ourselves but to him who has purchased us by the blood of the cross. We do know that this is a time of opportunity—and, if of opportunity, then of responsibility—for Evangelicals and Catholics to be Christians together in a way that helps prepare the world for the coming of him to whom belongs the kingdom, the power, and the glory forever. Amen.

Participants: Mr. Charles Colson (Prison Fellowship); Fr. Juan Diaz-Vilar, S.J. (Catholic Hispanic Ministries); Fr. Avery Dulles, S.J. (Fordham University); Bishop Francis George, OMI (Diocese of Yakima, Washington); Dr. Kent Hill (Eastern Nazarene College); Dr. Richard Land (Christian Life Commission of the Southern Baptist Convention); Dr. Larry Lewis (Home Mission Board of the Southern Baptist Convention); Dr. Jesse Miranda (Assemblies of God); Msgr. William Murphy (Chancellor of the Archdiocese of Boston); Fr. Richard John Neuhaus (Institute on Religion and Public Life); Mr. Brian O'Connell (World Evangelical Fellowship); Mr. Herbert Schlossberg (Fieldstead Foundation); Archbishop Francis Stafford (Archdiocese of Denver); Mr. George Weigel (Ethics and Public Policy Center); Dr. John White (Geneva College and the National Association of Evangelicals).

Endorsed by: Dr. William Abraham (Perkins School of Theology); Dr. Elizabeth Achtemeier (Union Theological Seminary, Virginia); Mr. William Bentley Ball (Harrisburg, Pennsylvania); Dr. Bill Bright (Campus Crusade for Christ); Professor Robert Destro (Catholic University of America); Fr. Augustine DiNoia, O.P. (Dominican House of Studies); Fr. Joseph P. Fitzpatrick, S.J. (Fordham University); Mr. Keith Fournier (American Center for Law and Justice); Bishop William Frey (Trinity Episcopal School for Ministry); Professor Mary Ann Glendon (Harvard Law School); Dr. Os Guinness (Trinity Forum); Dr. Nathan Hatch (University of Notre Dame); Dr. James Hitchcock (St. Louis University); Professor Peter Kreeft (Boston College); Fr. Matthew Lamb (Boston College); Mr. Ralph Martin (Renewal Ministries); Dr. Richard Mouw (Fuller Theological Seminary); Dr. Mark Noll (Wheaton College); Mr. Michael Novak (American Enterprise Institute); John Cardinal O'Connor (Archdiocese of New York); Dr. Thomas Oden (Drew University); Dr. James I. Packer (Regent College, British Columbia); The Rev. Pat Robertson (Regent University); Dr. John Rodgers (Trinity Episcopal School for Ministry); Bishop Carlos A. Sevilla, S.J. (Archdiocese of San Francisco).